HISTORIC HAUNTS OF SHREVEPORT

HISTORIC HAUNTS OF SHREVEPORT

GARY D. JOINER, PHD + CHERYL H. WHITE, PHD

Haunted America

Published by Haunted America
A Division of The History Press
Charleston, SC 29403
www.historypress.net

Cover image: Logan Mansion. *Photograph by Cheryl H. White.*

First published 2010

Manufactured in the United States

ISBN 978.1.59629.774.6

Library of Congress Cataloging-in-Publication Data
Joiner, Gary D.
Historic haunts of Shreveport / Gary D. Joiner and Cheryl H. White.
p. cm.
Includes bibliographical references.
ISBN 978-1-59629-774-6
1. Haunted places--Louisiana--Shreveport. 2. Ghosts--Louisiana--Shreveport. I. White, Cheryl H. II. Title.
BF1472.U6J657 2010
133.109763'99--dc22
2010027414

The authors dedicate this book to Dr. Willis P. Butler (1888–1991), the longest-serving public servant in Shreveport, whose ghost continues to show up for work occasionally.
May he long grace us with the unique visionary ethic of a true gentleman-physician.

CONTENTS

ACKNOWLEDGEMENTS

Many people have contributed energy, insight, inspiration and support for the final product that is *Historic Haunts of Shreveport*. The authors gratefully acknowledge: local historian Eric Brock for his pioneering work in telling Shreveport's story; Shawn Bohannon of the Louisiana State University at Shreveport, Noel Archives and Special Collections, for his interest and support of our detective work; graduate assistant Laura Beeman Nugent for help with research issues; Teal Buckner Lowring and Shelby Thoma for archival research; and the Louisiana Spirits Paranormal Investigators, especially Bess Maxwell, without whose serious dedication to this endeavor we would have lacked crucial evidence to enhance this work.

We acknowledge also the support of numerous friends and colleagues, as well as that of our spouses, Marilyn Segura Joiner and Paul S. White. For our students, we reserve a place of special thanks, for the enthusiasm and interest that drove them to walk cemeteries at night in the rain and mud and host Halloween parties at haunted mansions, and for their boundless curiosity that makes the job of a teaching historian worthwhile.

INTRODUCTION

Folklore and history bear little resemblance to each other, yet they often relate in unique and unexpected ways. As a general category, folklore encompasses the cultural phenomenon known as the local ghost story, and every community has its own locally branded version of this. These stories are the tales of people and collective experiences that survive almost solely on oral tradition—the operative word, tradition, often excludes the application of the historical discipline. Ghost stories are a form of lore that relies upon oral tradition; indeed, the repeated telling of these tales not only derives from but also contributes to the overall culture of a specific area and its people.

Like most folklore, word of mouth is the primary means of perpetuation of ghost stories, and any attribution to a historical source is unnecessary and may in fact be cumbersome and unwelcomed. Yet they are rich manifestations of a shared social understanding in communities around the world, extending far back into human history. They are the traditional stock of slumber parties, campfires and party conversations, and even the skeptics may be quick to admit that a chilling ghost story is as good as any other fiction—with the added attraction of the possibility of brushing against that which we cannot hope to understand.

It is worth noting that much of Shreveport's "haunted history" depends, at least partially, on firsthand accounts of people who have personally experienced the paranormal or, more commonly, know someone who has. This distinction is important. Folklore doesn't necessarily require a story to be true. It is important to know whether the person relating the tale assumes it is true. When someone believes a ghost story to be true, it is a legend. If not, it is a tale. There is a general expectation that the teller of the *tale* will exaggerate. However, legends survive, not because the historian can verify them, but because they are often convincing in their authenticity derived from strong oral tradition.[1]

Adolescents and teens are known to relate both legends and tales. Who has not heard of giggling and adventurous teenagers who enjoy exploring the haunted sites of their own communities? Perhaps this is how our preoccupation with the "world beyond" arises or is an indication of our struggle to deal collectively with issues of our own mortality. Ghost stories and tales fascinate and fire the imaginations because, if true, the life beyond this one seems even more intriguing.

Many ghost stories share a striking similarity, no matter where they originate. A review of folklore throughout the country and, indeed, throughout the world reveals their common threads. For instance, there was a common belief among the ancients that ghosts haunted crossroads, a symbolic expression of those people's attempts to understand the afterlife. It is an interesting observation that some of the most popular twenty-first-century ghost lore involves railroad crossings or highway intersections. Indeed, just such a story exists in the tale of this north Louisiana community.

Many other traditional markers of the modern ghost story have ancient origins. The common belief that ghosts appear at night and not during the day is so frequent a part of ghost stories that no one questions this. Another common theme for ghost lore involves the attempt to determine why the dead do not move on to the afterlife or why they insist on returning to an earthly existence. Throughout the ages, several explanations have been given in folklore. Some return to settle unfinished business—either with loved ones or with enemies. Others return to the scene of their brutal or violent deaths to help bring those responsible to justice. Still others return to comfort those who grieve.[2]

The lack of a proper burial has been enough cause to unsettle the dead, as has the disruption of one's eternal resting place. There are profound psychological origins of this ghostly attribution, as burial ceremonies and rituals have been part of the human experience since prehistory. Such ritual provides closure to the human existence, and the ceremony and commemoration of mortal remains of the dead marks its finality. It is logical, therefore, that grave desecrations or improper burial rituals would carry the connotation of disrupting the ordered human process of dealing with death. Therefore, if a person dies and is given a burial in a suitable place and with comforting ceremonies, that person is not likely to appear as a ghost. However, a person who has had an unconventional burial or no burial at all, or whose burial site has been desecrated, is more likely to be the main character in a ghost story. Obviously, among these various explanations are benevolent as well as malevolent reasons for ghosts to return to haunt the living, if indeed such a thing has ever occurred outside of legend or tale.

Shreveport, Louisiana, has a history and culture uniquely shaped by its geography and diverse population. As early as 1819, the state legislature in Louisiana explored the best way to address a major obstacle to commercial development of its new state—a "Great Raft" of debris on the Red River that made the regional waterway unfit for use. Because interstate commerce seemed the core issue, the State of Louisiana looked to the federal government for assistance with this problem in northwest and central Louisiana. This "Great Raft" inhibited settlement and commerce at a time when the United States was intent on exploring the full potential of lands acquired during the recent Louisiana Purchase. Within just a few years, navigation of the waterway was possible, and the project's chief engineer, Captain Henry Miller Shreve, wrote to Congress, "There are now many flourishing cotton plantations on the river where the lands were nearly all inundated by the back water. A town sprung up equal in population and surpassing any on the Red River in the amount of business."[3]

The settlement Shreve referred to would bear his name—first as Shreve Town and then Shreveport, even though he and his family never lived there. People flocked to the banks of the newly unencumbered river to seek their livelihoods and carve out futures in the new land, which was occupied by tribes of the Caddo Indians. The first streets of the settlement lauded the heroes of the recently established Republic of Texas, including Travis, Crockett and Fannin. Indeed, the city's main thoroughfare, Texas Street, honored the Republic of Texas itself. The city grew out from the river back to the west, and by the middle of the nineteenth century, it boasted a growing population with significant urban and residential development underway. From its early days, the economy of Shreveport depended upon several types of activity, all inextricably linked to one another. Merchants provided goods for the planters and farmers of a three-state region (Louisiana, Arkansas and Texas) and made extensive use of the river as a highway for transportation of those goods. The booming cotton trade benefited steamboats and cotton brokers, as well as creditors who financed these transactions. The economic health of the city of Shreveport therefore defined itself in the activity on the Red River. From its earliest days, Shreveport has offered tales and legend surrounding some of the city's most significant landmarks and personalities.

Like all communities with many generations of history, Shreveport has witnessed all the hallmarks of passing time and recorded those observations in the rich tapestry of its own local lore. Inevitably, what has emerged from the pages that transect both history and folklore are the often sensational but persistent tales of the paranormal variety—complete with ghostly apparitions, hauntings and other accounts of unexplained phenomena. It is no accident that these accounts share a universal theme, that they are centered on some of Shreveport's most enduring sites and most influential places and people. Taken together, these tales share the singular binding thread of a city's past. Shreveport's haunted history reflects varying eras, personalities and contexts that collectively produced both history and folklore. At times, the two seem interchangeable, and indeed, sometimes history can prove the legend.

Like all southern and western cities in the nineteenth century, Shreveport faced massive challenges. Trauma and tragedy, as well as economic boom and prosperity, came in alternating cycles. Within fifteen years of its founding, Shreveport had transformed itself from a crude frontier outpost to a bustling river port. Trails and traces gave way to roads connecting the young town with other settlements in the region, particularly to those in eastern Texas. Steamboat commerce made Shreveport a major cotton market. Farmers brought their harvest to wholesalers who then transshipped the valuable bales downstream to New Orleans. Cattlemen drove their herds along the Texas Trail and through Shreveport's Texas Street to the riverside, where they were loaded on steamboats for markets all along the Mississippi River Valley. The city's heavy reliance on river and rail transport meant that the increasing national sectionalism of the 1850s brought a real threat to the young city's economic security. The Red River and the incomplete rail system beginning to link inland areas in the region both brought new ideas with them. As the South moved toward severing ties with the North, Shreveport was forced to adapt. Political rhetoric, both for secession and cooperation with northern markets, competed with each other. The Civil War brought new challenges as the state of Louisiana moved the capital temporarily to Shreveport. The long conflict left Shreveport intact, not suffering the devastation of other southern cities. Its population rapidly expanded while the physical size of the town did not. Informal suburbs allowed the city to grow. Shreveport discovered that it was not immune to urban problems.

The city was plagued by diseases common in the South. A tragic and devastating yellow fever epidemic in 1873 left Shreveport ill-equipped to deal with the mounting death toll. In haste to stop the spread of the illness, the city quickly disposed of many of the victims in one mass grave in a local cemetery. Since that time, the lore surrounding Oakland Cemetery and reported encounters with ghosts of these yellow fever victims has persisted. Yet the haunting of Oakland Cemetery, like the others to be explored in these pages, actually represents yet another way to tell the unique history of a city that has witnessed much—and survived. In an interesting intersection of historical discipline and paranormal inquiry, the process of producing this work actually resulted in historians witnessing the investigation of Oakland Cemetery by paranormal experts for the first time.

With the arrival of the twentieth century, Shreveport mirrored the rest of the nation, in step with major political movements and economic trends. The 1920s represented economic boom. The oil and gas industry brought economic security for the region and created wealth for a segment of the city's population. The architecture of this decade reflected the confident prosperity in Shreveport through buildings like the Caddo Parish Courthouse, the Municipal Auditorium and C.E. Byrd High School—all with ghostly lore attached to them. Each of these buildings is significant in its own right as part of Shreveport's culture, regardless of ghost stories attached to it. Like other local ghost stories, the tale involving the haunting of Byrd High School has a few variations, one with obscure origins and one firmly based on the historical record. The same is true for both the courthouse and the Municipal Auditorium.

The 1930s saw the impact of the Great Depression. Thanks to Shreveport's diverse economy, including the construction of Barksdale Field—later to become Barksdale Air Force Base—a thriving cotton trade and nearby producing oil and gas wells, Shreveport fared better than some cities of similar size. Other construction projects of this era included a new federal building, the Texas Street Bridge over the Red River connecting to Bossier City and the Louisiana State Exhibit Museum. It was a time of construction and growth amid the backdrop of economic downturn that struck many places across the country more severely.

The 1940s brought the specter of war home to Shreveport and the region in general. While Barksdale was a real and visible sign of the area's national importance, other landmarks have a more provincial significance in our history and tales of haunting. Some of Shreveport's most striking landmarks are home to tales of the paranormal. Twentieth-century Shreveport has the distinction of being home to the "Cradle of the Stars" of the popular radio program *Louisiana Hayride* at the Municipal Auditorium. This famous stage was home to an unknown Elvis Presley in the mid-1950s, as well as artists such as Johnny Cash and Hank Williams. All of these men went on to make music history, and their legacy lives on in this historic place that launched their meteoric careers. Paralleling the historic nature of the building are the stories of those individuals that involve tales of the paranormal. The Municipal Auditorium in Shreveport has been the site of numerous paranormal investigations, and it has been the subject of a national television documentary recounting the stories of its haunting.

Ghost stories do not always involve old buildings, mansions or cemeteries. Sometimes the strong personality of a prominent individual continues to live on in ghostly lore or legend. One persistent and related legend is that of a Caddo Parish coroner who still frequents multiple public sites. Because Dr. Willis Butler's public service was such a prominent part of Shreveport civic and social life throughout the twentieth century, he deserves his own chapter, which relates an unusually advanced approach to medicine and social ills. Furthermore, the dedication of this book to Dr. Butler expresses esteem for a man who is the longest-serving public official in Shreveport history, especially since many believe he continues to appear at the Caddo Parish Courthouse.

For most people, the archetype of the "spooky old mansion" is the epitome of a haunted place. The allure of this stereotypical old haunted house is universal and easily understood. Not only is an old house a veritable depository of its own history, but the structure itself also can preserve the memory of those who once lived there, laughed and loved within its walls. Human nature often finds fascination in the lives of those now gone, with only a portrait or personal effects to prove that they ever existed.

Grand old homes of some of the city's most important families have become the subject of haunted tales. Historical investigators find the human story of the era and the families reexamined as tales of the supernatural world. Old buildings always reflect the lives of the people who once lived there. This book details the haunting at two of Shreveport's grand old homes—the Logan Mansion and the Davis Homeplace. These are interesting subjects for investigation, not just because they are part of ghost lore but also because they are important landmarks in Shreveport history. Sometimes historical inquiry reveals inconsistencies, if not untruths, about the persistent legends surrounding these grand homes, but this usually does not dampen enthusiasm for these tales of the paranormal.

Other local ghost stories do not originate with real people or even real events. Indeed, sometimes they represent nothing more than a common cultural expression that is mysteriously consistent in many diverse settings. In one of the city's most persistent ghost legends, the Forbing Ghost, the historical investigation yields an interesting sociological finding. This story is linked to common railroad lore found in numerous cities across the United States. Most of these railroad ghost stories are exactly alike, as common as the rails themselves.

The harshness or brutality of the past is also expressed in lore, perhaps as a way of diffusing its reality or healing the pain of great human tragedy. Another legendary haunted site is the old Caddo Correctional Center or Penal Farm, where the hardships of the lives of prisoners in the Louisiana state correctional system provide fodder for ghost stories. Many places throughout the South instituted a harsh, agriculturally based penal system in the late nineteenth century, a prison structure many analysts claim represented little more than a new form of slavery. Conditions in all Louisiana prisons were harsh by national standards into the twentieth century. The abandoned Caddo Parish Penal Farm site echoes memories of a less enlightened time in history, and the ghost tales there abound.

Within easy driving distance of Shreveport is the historic Mansfield battleground, site of a Civil War battle where Union troops attempted to capture Shreveport (then capital of Louisiana) as part of a maneuver into Texas. Battlegrounds always provide rich stories of their own, separate from any ghostly soldiers still wandering the area. Ghosts of war dead are among the most common depictions in legends and tales across the centuries of recorded history. Those who die in the service of a greater cause exemplify self-sacrifice that can spark ghost tales that embody humanity's desire to keep the sacrifice of the soldier alive.

Any reader seeking ghost stories to tell by campfires or at slumber parties should take warning. What follows here is history. Woven into the pages of history are stories that are a means by which local culture has attempted to honor the past through legend and lore. *Historic Haunts of Shreveport* is not an attempt to retell old haunted folklore in the hope of arriving at concrete solutions for mysterious events and occurrences involving these notable Shreveport sites and landmarks. The authors are professional historians who think it best to leave the business of the paranormal to those who study it. This book is not an attempt to convince anyone that ghosts are real, for that is an exercise that reaches beyond the scope and limitation of the historian. Historians believe in the energy of the past, and the ghosts of history are real enough in this sense.

Beyond these cautionary disclaimers, the popular appeal of this rich folklore provides historians with the chance to frame the true story of a city within the intriguing twist of the paranormal. *Historic Haunts of Shreveport* is primarily the history of one city in the southern United States, shaped by people and external events, by acts of God as well as accidents of fate. Each chapter carefully reflects both the pertinent history of a remarkable city and its people, tempered with just enough of the supernatural to kindle the imagination. This is a history of Shreveport written to include mystery and intrigue, offered to the reader with the assumption that everyone enjoys a great ghost story.

OAKLAND CEMETERY

Nothing is more stereotypically considered haunted than an old cemetery. By day, they are peaceful resting places for those who have passed on by day, but by night, they can be creepy, scary places where imaginations can run wild. This is especially true with graves that lie within old iron gates from a long-forgotten time and that represent the lives of some of the most influential, fascinating and tragic figures of Shreveport's history. Historic Oakland Cemetery is located near two other haunted landmarks of Shreveport, the Logan Mansion and the Municipal Auditorium. A stroll through this area at night produces the perfect haunted tour for the visitor or native who wants to experience the history of the city in a supernatural way.

Oakland Cemetery is a picturesque spot, with expansive old oak and cedar trees and a landscape accentuated by gentle rolling hills. Scattered throughout are the typical Victorian-era monuments, including statues, obelisks, slabs and iron fences. People of this Shreveport neighborhood once thought nothing of walking through this beautiful landscape for leisure or even perhaps spreading out a picnic blanket on a warm spring day. Indeed, many in the neighborhood still do this occasionally. It is a perfect spot for the living to commune with the dead or simply to remember them in quiet moments of respect and reflection.

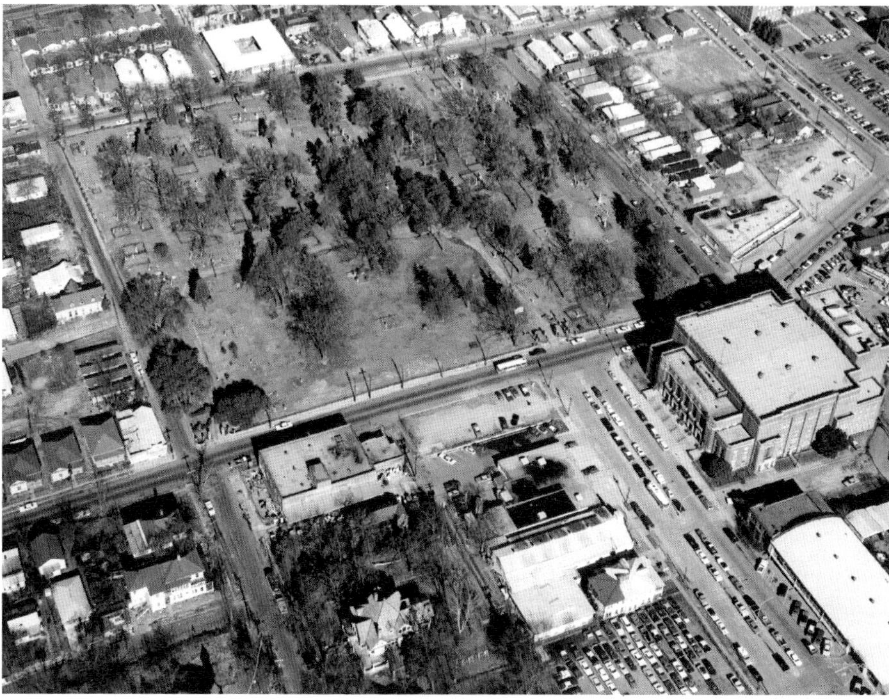

Aerial view of Oakland Cemetery, including the Municipal Auditorium (at right) and the Logan Mansion (at lower center). *Courtesy of Archives and Special Collections, Louisiana State University in Shreveport.*

Some people believe ghosts are a representation of residual energy from personalities and the imprints they leave behind. For them, Oakland Cemetery is haunted by virtue of those who made this scenic spot their final home. At perpetual rest within Oakland Cemetery are Confederate soldiers, mayors, the famous Shreveport madam Annie McCune and important early settlers of the Shreveport-Bossier area on the Red River. A walk among the graves reveals a who's who of early Shreveport, including such notables as Mary Bennett Cane, wife of James Cane and considered the mother of Shreveport and Bossier City. Also in Oakland is Dr. Alphonse Smith, the first African American physician in Shreveport. Colonel Leon Marks, a hero at Vicksburg during the Civil War, rests here as well.

Burials began in Shreveport in 1840, even though the city did not officially establish the cemetery until 1847. By mayoral decree, Lawrence Pike Crain that year required that all bodies buried within Shreveport

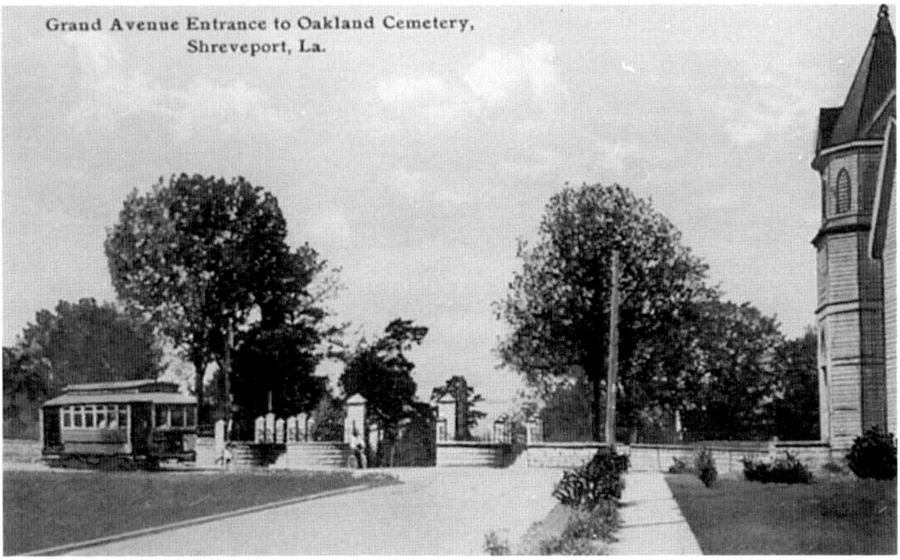

Postcard of the Grand Avenue main entrance to Oakland Cemetery, with St. Paul's Methodist Church at right. *Collection of Gary D. Joiner.*

should be placed in Oakland Cemetery. As a result, some bodies buried prior to this time were moved.[4] The oldest verified burial in Oakland was that of Rufus Sewall, the second mayor of Shreveport, who was killed in a duel in 1842. Disturbance of those who were previously ritually buried is a frequently cited reason in folklore for cemetery haunting. The premise is that moving an interred body disrupts the rest and can summon the soul to its earthly existence. The city sold burial plots in Oakland until 1930.[5] Today, the cemetery has been the victim of both neglect and malicious property damage, although dedicated preservationists work diligently to maintain this remarkable reminder of the past.

Why ghosts haunt cemeteries would have obvious answers for those who believe in such phenomena. For Shreveport, this sacred ground represents a history classroom of sorts, eternally imprinted with the lives of the city's past. Dates and names carved in stone are much more than simple markers of a life that once was; they are also living memorials of Shreveport history. So many of those who lie in Oakland Cemetery could be a chapter of their own in the great story of the city, so significant were their contributions to the unique flavor and allure of the city by the Red River. Notably, Oakland Cemetery is the final resting place for approximately eight hundred victims of the city's yellow fever epidemic of 1873.[6] The death toll mounted so rapidly during that fateful summer that city officials did not have time to arrange for timely proper burials. A mass grave is now marked with a simple monument commemorating the numerous dead who share eternal rest in a common plot of consecrated ground. According to supernatural legend and lore, this abrupt and hasty burial does not allow the soul proper closure as it passes from one realm of existence to the next. This speaks to the haunted tales that surround Oakland Cemetery.

There is more to the Oakland mystique. Jews escaping the anti-Semitism of Europe in the early nineteenth century came in large numbers to the South, and many settled in and around the booming Shreveport area. The Hebrew Mutual Benevolent Association purchased a tract of ground within Oakland in 1859 and dedicated its use as the

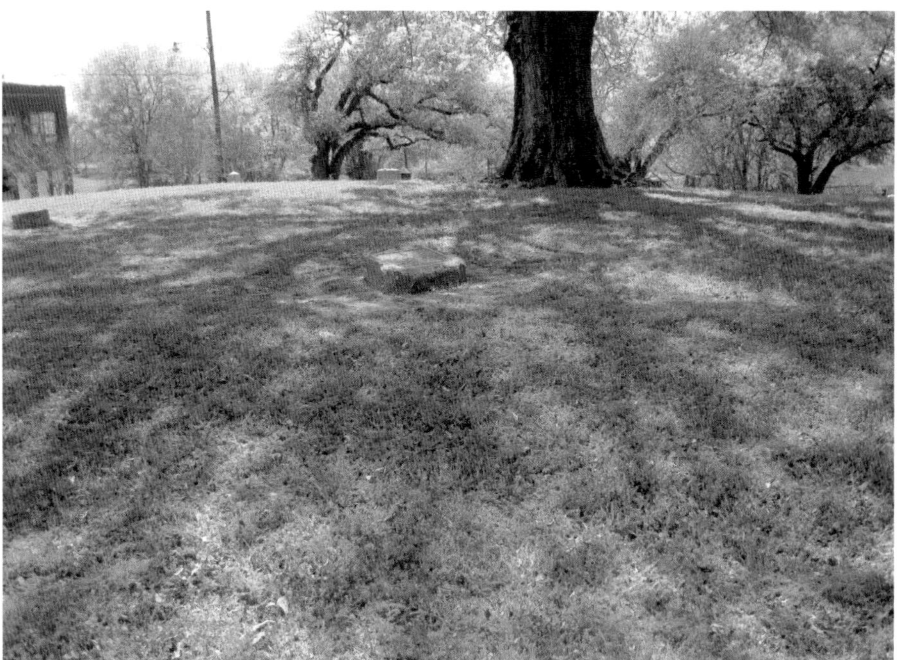

The yellow fever mound in Oakland Cemetery. *Photograph by Cheryl H. White.*

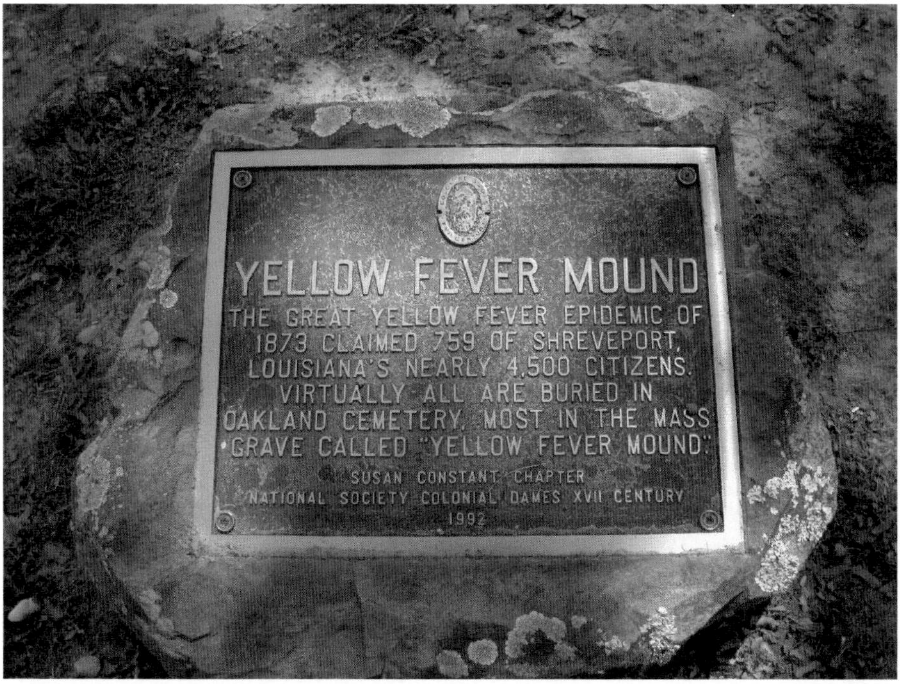

The bronze memorial marker on the yellow fever mound in Oakland Cemetery. *Photograph by Cheryl H. White.*

first burial place for Jews within the city.[7] This one-acre plot is a poignant reminder even today of the number of Jews who sought new lives and refuge in this part of the world during times of great persecution.

The energy of history lives on, and many believe this to be true in the lore of haunted cemeteries. After all, cemeteries do not really exist for the dead but for the living who wish to remember them. Some believe that merely walking through a cemetery evokes an awareness of one's own mortality, heightening the senses and awareness. This makes all of the legends of the haunted cemetery true in a universal sense, since the subconscious human mind reacts and responds to the encounter with the permanence of death.[8]

Some paranormal authors contend that cemeteries are likely to be the least haunted places of all, since souls freed from the physical constraints of their decaying and deteriorating bodies would remain, especially in relation to a mortal body that is no longer of any use.[9]

What then explains the sudden chill experienced by those who visit the cemetery or night or the strange and soft murmurings heard by visitors during the day, in absence of cemetery personnel or other people nearby? If actual ghosts do indeed haunt Oakland, who are they likely to be? The paranormal investigative group Louisiana Spirits places special importance on the yellow fever mound, as such tragic historic circumstances would contribute to the unrest of many souls. A recent investigation by that team focused on the yellow fever mound, which, ironically, represents one of the most scenic parts of the old graveyard.

In the summer of 1873, Shreveport experienced a horrific epidemic of yellow fever, as did other places throughout Louisiana. It was the worst epidemic the city ever experienced, even though yellow fever had visited twice before. An estimated one-third of area residents may have fled Shreveport before the official quarantine became effective.[10] Early chroniclers and scientists have cited various causes as the origin of this particular infection, ranging from the wreck of a steamboat—the *Ruby*, which sank at the mouth of Cross Bayou while carrying one hundred head of cattle—to the introduction of the disease through a traveling circus company from Mexico.[11] Immediately following the epidemic, medical attention focused on the city's apparently poor drainage systems and infamous lack of cleanliness. An official report written by a group of physicians shortly after the epidemic ceased noted, "The fact seems to be overlooked that this condition of this city has always existed, and while on general hygienic ground, want of cleanliness may foster and render more malignant the disease when once introduced, there is no evidence that filth and garbage…have ever, by themselves, generated yellow fever."[12]

Other theories of origin focused on the clearing of the Red River Raft. This theory was debunked because, of the estimated one hundred men employed during the season to continue to clear debris on the Red River, there was not a single reported case of yellow fever among them. The investigative committee concluded that the origin of the epidemic was importation from Cuba to New Orleans and then to Shreveport from the Red River. The committee also noted the disparity of racial infections, with whites affected mortally nearly six times as often as blacks, and with the greatest mortality occurring in men between the ages of twenty and thirty-five years.[13]

Yellow fever was a frequent annual summer visitor to Louisiana and claimed more than a few victims each season, but the 1873 occurrence was especially virulent. The port city of New Orleans suffered more often than most Louisiana locales due to the obvious international contact of both humans and cargo. The riverboats were obvious means of transmission, but the railroads no doubt contributed to the spread of the pestilence during times of high infection rates.[14] Throughout the eighteenth and nineteenth centuries, Louisiana witnessed wave after wave of recurrences, so the scale of the Shreveport epidemic seems almost inevitable in this historical context.

Today, scientists have an understanding of the origins and spread of the infection. It is a virus; more specifically, a flavivirus, spread by mosquitoes. Among related organisms, this particular virus is not especially strong, unable to live outside a human host for more than an hour or two. Transmission is comparatively difficult, and it rarely mutates as other viruses frequently do. To have been one of the most dreaded of illnesses in the United States, its modern scientific description does not sound terribly impressive. Yet it was the origin of a fear and generalized panic in cities affected by it on an unparalleled scale.[15]

In the early stages of yellow fever, the victim suffers with headache and fever, followed by a brief symptom-free period, during which time a great number of victims spontaneously recover. However, many more progress to the third phase of the illness, known as the "intoxication" stage, when organ failure begins to occur, progressing typically to delirium, coma and death. Medical science knows today that transmission occurs through mosquitoes and that it can be transmitted from infected humans back to a new mosquito host and then to another human, creating a cycle of perpetual infection. This explains its prevalence during the summer months, particularly in southern and tropical climes.[16] Even today, any resident of Shreveport can provide convincing testimony of the mosquito population during the hottest months of the year.

One can only imagine the impact of the epidemic on the citizens of the city, who most certainly reacted with disbelief and fear. The clergy were indispensable allies to the physicians in this tragic scenario, and in Shreveport, five Roman Catholic priests and two religious sisters heroically died in the service and care of the city's dying victims. Furthermore, many other local ministers and pastors remained and worked among the sick and dying, even opening up their churches to serve as hospitals. Another hero who succumbed to the fever was U.S. Army first lieutenant Eugene Augustus Woodruff, the commander of the engineering unit tasked with clearing the Great Raft. The logjam had reappeared in 1872, and Congress wanted the Red River opened for commerce. Woodruff and his men had made great progress when the fever struck. The army ordered the unit to leave Shreveport for its own safety, but Woodruff remained to help the people of Shreveport in their time of need. He sent his men, including his brother George, to supposedly healthier areas near Alexandria. He died at 9:00 p.m. on September 29, 1873, working with the priests to care for victims. The heat and the death during that summer of 1873 tried the resolve and faith of the young river city, perhaps best reflected in that single mass grave at Oakland Cemetery.

The epidemic in Shreveport and the ensuing application of drastic measures attracted national attention. The September 30, 1873 edition of the *New York Times* reported on the mass burials, with the following poignant update from a citizen witness: "Several of the most prominent and useful citizens of Shreveport have fallen victim to the epidemic… the population fearfully thinned out by sickness and death. We no longer have funerals."[17] This speaks directly to the desperation that forced a disregard for common courtesies of proper burial rites.

The witness in this article noted that there were already four hundred dead in Shreveport, with another seven hundred or more infected and ill with the disease. The city seemingly shut down, stalled to a stop because of fear of the spread of the infection and a rapid loss of the supporting workforce. The witness made the following surreal description: "The hearses, followed by one or two carriages, dash through the streets like a section of artillery in a battle seeking a position."[18]

Throughout the nineteenth century, the origin and exact means of transmission of yellow fever seemed to lay beyond the understanding of medical science, evidenced by official inquiry reports published in medical journals of the time. However, the disease held a strong religious significance, as did all the great plagues of history, because afflicted people in their helplessness traditionally look for spiritual meanings and divine purpose. Before his death in the Civil War, Episcopal bishop Leonidas K. Polk had prepared a special prayer during the yellow fever epidemics of the 1850s for the entire Episcopal Diocese of Louisiana to use in just such future circumstances. "Turn from us the ravage of pestilence," the bishop wrote, implying and recognizing the sovereign will of God in the great confusion of disease epidemic.[19]

For more than a century, yellow fever turned up unexpectedly and stayed for varying periods of time, but never with more startling ferocity than the summer of 1873. This epidemic entered the city's general awareness on or about August 27 of that year and continued until late October, spanning a period of just over eight weeks of virulent infection.[20] At the end of the epidemic, which abated with as much mystery as it had arrived, Shreveport was left staggering at the cost. A single mass grave at Oakland Cemetery expresses the helplessness and inability of a city to deal with death on such a massive scale.

So is this great tragedy in Shreveport history the origin of the haunting of Oakland Cemetery? Investigators noted measurable paranormal activity around the yellow fever mound, including unusual spikes in electromagnetic field measurements. One witness reported feeling a distinct "cold spot" near the top of the mass grave mound. More than one witness recounts hearing murmuring voices, as if carried on the gentle wind through the massive old oak trees that anchor the cemetery grounds. The question of whether it is only a passing wind or whispers of the dead must be left to the discernment of the individual, either paranormal believer or skeptic.

The question persists about why cemeteries would be haunted at all, for the location of the human remains is not likely to be an attractive destination for a disembodied soul that conceivably could visit a variety of other earthly locales. It seems unlikely that a buried human body, minus its soul, would attempt to rise or escape from the grave, although that is one commonly related tale of at least one grave within Oakland. The tomb of twenty-two-year-old Cora Lee Wilson, buried in Oakland in the late 1800s, continually has been the site of a "mysterious" removal of bricks near the foot, with her tiny coffin clearly visible inside. Is this the result of her soul/body attempting to escape, or is it only the malicious vandalism of opportunistic visitors who wish to perpetuate the cemetery's haunted reputation?

Why would a ghost visit his or her own grave? Such a destination for haunting hardly seems to hold much appeal, at least to the human understanding. What becomes apparent in the examination of other ghost stories throughout the city is a clear pattern of returning to the familiar places that once held great meaning in life. Therefore, homes, favorite buildings, workplaces, playgrounds or other sites of significance are all understandable locales for ghostly visitations. Yet somehow, the allure of the graveyard is hardest of all to grasp, except when viewed in the framework of human culture and historical expressions of the importance of the rituals used to mark life and death.

The explanation for this lies with the funeral and burial rituals of our collective human experience that are prehistoric in origin. Humans mourn their dead, ritualize their passing and commemorate the closure and finality of life with proper burial. These practices are literally thousands of years old, reflecting a common human understanding throughout history that it is through such rituals and preservation of earthly remains that human mortality is marked and understood to the extent possible. To bury the dead and mark the location of their bodies with stones and flowers is to acknowledge that this life was indeed worth living. Gravestones stand for decades and centuries to remember the life that once was temporal now exists in an eternal realm of memory. Therefore, it is accurate to note that cemeteries are for the living, but even experts cannot know the impact of such ritualistic closure on the life abruptly ended.

For the victims of the Shreveport yellow fever epidemic, such common and necessary ritualistic measures did not apply. Contemporary accounts reveal with stunning clarity the hastiness of the bodies' removals, as well as the desperate attempts to dispose of the bodies in fear of perpetuating the alarming infection rate. The souls of 715 of the city's residents now lie together communally in a solemn and sad expression of a helpless attempt to understand the incomprehensible events of the summer of 1873.

MUNICIPAL AUDITORIUM

In 1929 on Grand Avenue in downtown Shreveport, a new and extravagant entertainment venue opened to the public. The Municipal Auditorium has a fascinating history and has made an indelible impact on the culture of the entire nation, and, some contend, the entire world. The structure opened as a place for entertainment, theatrical performances, sporting events and a variety of other activities that might require the spacious hall with three thousand seats and over six thousand square feet. As a city structure, it also has been home to various agencies and served other functions throughout its history. Among these are the Early Aircraft Warning System (precursor to RADAR), the Girl Scouts of America and the Mid-South Wrestling Federation. The structure was also a billeting station for World War II soldiers and a temporary home for the Shreveport city morgue. The history of this Shreveport landmark is so diverse that a ghost hunter might find it difficult to decide where to begin to explore its lore and legend. The building itself is an expression of the city's history and has been shaped by changing culture and social patterns that transformed the city in the decades of the twentieth century.

The massive and dated structure of the Municipal Auditorium is not easily at home with the conservative design of the present-day city

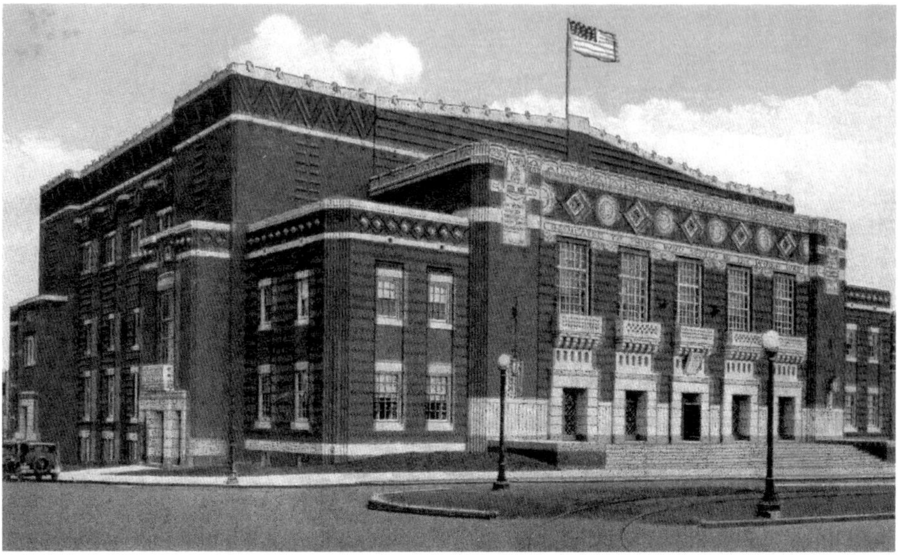

Undated postcard of the Municipal Auditorium from the 1930s. *Collection of Gary D. Joiner.*

landscape and, therefore, is an easily recognizable landmark in downtown Shreveport. Located near to two other notable haunted locations, the Logan Mansion and Oakland Cemetery, the Municipal Auditorium's construction was nevertheless quite at home in this old section of the city at the time its construction began. Observers of the 1920s did not deem the lavish Art Deco–style architecture of the building as extravagant in its day; indeed, its attraction was that it spoke directly to the fun and folly of the Roaring Twenties in a quite tangible way. All over America and Europe, this unique style of architecture expressed the fun and frenetic vitality of the age.

Conceived as a visible testament to Shreveport's prosperity on the eve of the Great Depression, the Municipal Auditorium and its five stories of brick, mortar and limestone echo many whispers of the past. The decade of the 1920s found Shreveport with a strong economy as one of the primary centers of the oil industry for the nation. The student of history should expect that the conditions of the age would find expression in architecture and design of significant public structures. In this regard, the Municipal Auditorium lives up to the expectation.

Following World War I, the nation's economy saw tremendous expansion in the Roaring Twenties. Shreveport continued to benefit from its unique geography, which permitted river commerce and fixed the city as a focal point for travelers going any direction in the region. In addition, the city benefited from its proximity to fertile oil fields and the prosperity they generated.

The 1920s uniquely manifested in Shreveport through an oil boom that led the city's economy for decades to come. It was a time of cultural dynamism, and the expanding city population and upscale demographic demanded an appropriate artistic venue. Construction of the Municipal Auditorium began amid one of the most optimistic and prosperous decades in all of American history. The building today still reflects a bygone era. This was a time when American cities became truly urban and commercial, and Shreveport was a model of the age.

Today, the Municipal Auditorium enjoys the mysterious reputation as, perhaps, one of the most haunted places in all of the American South, a fact attested to by many paranormal professionals. Its place in history is assured by some rather unique cultural and musical contributions as well as by its paranormal affiliations. There are few public places in the United States that offer as much fodder for ghost hunters of any variety, for the Municipal Auditorium has witnessed triumph and acclaim as well as sadness and death. Indeed, one of the most fascinating aspects of the history of the Municipal Auditorium lies in the fact that it has been home to so many functions and events that its haunted nature could originate at almost any point.

Although the facility served as home to many cultural events in its eighty-year lifetime, undoubtedly the most remarkable aspect of its story is in its affiliation with the famous *Louisiana Hayride*. Beginning in 1948 as a weekly radio program, the *Hayride* attracted young and ambitious artists from the emerging country music scene. The radio program provided a widespread audience and an amateur stage, something that proved to be a magical combination for many young musicians. By the mid-1950s, the stage at the Municipal Auditorium had seen performances by such country greats as Johnny Cash, Hank Williams and George Jones. However, the most famous entertainer

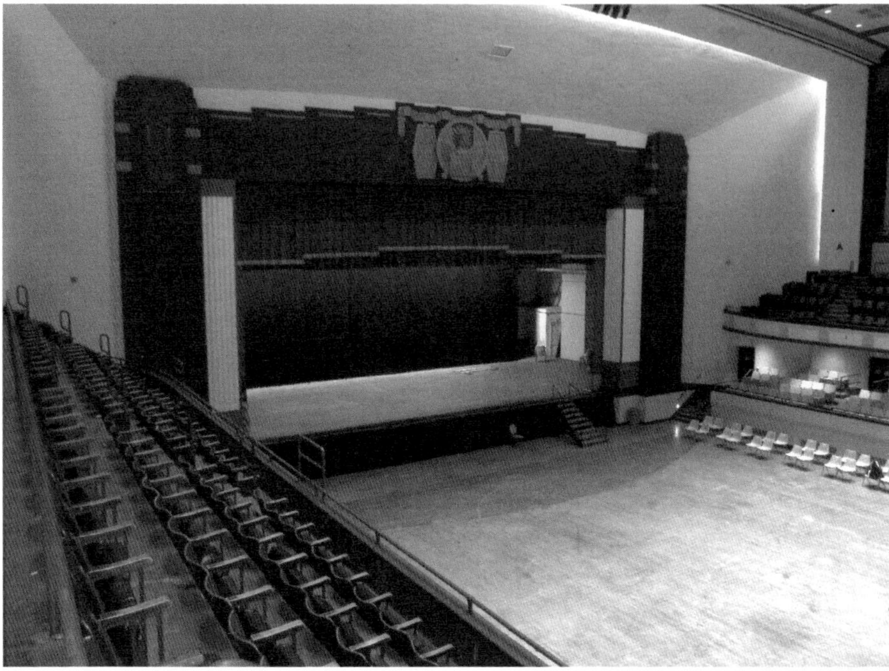

Stage at the Municipal Auditorium seen from the upper balcony. *Photograph by Gary D. Joiner.*

associated with the Municipal Auditorium first stepped on the *Hayride* stage on October 18, 1954. This nineteen-year-old with an unusual musical sound was Elvis Aaron Presley.

By the following year, Elvis Presley was under contract to appear weekly on the *Hayride*, and his career was soaring. His contracted rate of eighteen dollars per week seems laughable to present-day readers, but it is a poignant reminder of the humble origins of some of the most fascinating figures in history.[21] The contributions of Elvis Presley to popular culture, music and twentieth-century society are unassailable from any perspective. Shreveport is proud to claim that Elvis launched his career from the *Louisiana Hayride*, and as a result, the Municipal Auditorium stands as an iconic image of this unique contribution to musical and cultural history. It was from the stage of the *Louisiana Hayride* that KWKH Radio made a now-famous statement to a group of clamoring fans: "Elvis has left the building."[22] To commemorate this claim to international music history, the city of Shreveport renamed historic Grand Avenue as Elvis Presley Boulevard.

The arrival of Elvis Presley to the pages of music history is an event that has few comparable parallels. The power of commercial radio as a popular medium in the mid-twentieth century, punctuated by the rapidly spreading popularity of country music, came together in a unique historical manner on a stage in Shreveport, Louisiana. The rise of media in American history assumes a completely new relevance when examined in light of the *Louisiana Hayride*. The broadcast of the *Louisiana Hayride* changed American popular culture in a significant way and launched a new form of music heard by millions.

In the post–World War II era, another period of booming economy and peaceful prosperity settled over America. Radio was the primary medium for entertainment and news well into the early part of the 1960s. This statement is perhaps most true for areas of the South, where predominantly agricultural and rural populations provided a ready audience for the emerging country music sound before the genre gained the overwhelming popularity that it readily enjoys today. The *Louisiana Hayride* was unique because it sought out new talent and provided a stage and a radio forum for the unknowns. The radio station KWKH enjoyed the benefit of a strong signal, reaching listeners in at least twenty-eight states.[23]

The *Louisiana Hayride* was so popular that it drew large crowds to hear the show live at the Municipal Auditorium, with many attendees coming from outlying areas. Surely the imprint of these regional and national visitors brought with them another layer of history from the Municipal Auditorium. In the process, Shreveport became a necessary stopping point on the way to country music stardom for hopeful amateurs. They all expected to follow the same path traveled by Hank Williams, who went from the *Hayride* straight to the Grand Ole Opry in Nashville and into the pages of country music history.[24]

As the home of such significant music history, the *Louisiana Hayride* enjoyed a prestigious reputation and a devoted following throughout the decade of the 1950s and into the 1960s before succumbing to the growing impact of the emerging medium of television. As radio lost its allure to the households of America, so did its programming, despite the level of popularity it once enjoyed. The *Hayride* gradually declined from a weekly program to a quarterly program before ending its first era in history in 1969. Although there have been two revival attempts in succeeding decades of the twentieth century, the *Louisiana Hayride* clearly belongs to the era of Elvis Presley, Johnny Cash, Hank Williams and other notables.

Because of its rich and diverse functions throughout the history of Shreveport, the Municipal Auditorium's walls could surely speak to the tales of the past. Shreveport's booming economy and positioning as a major crossroads for the four-state region drew thousands to the city, many of whom stayed. Standing in the enormous spaces within the structure, one can easily imagine the laughter, applause and music, from a 1950s *Louisiana Hayride* stage to a classical concert, a wrestling match or a regal community pageant. One might consider the faces and anxieties of men gathering to leave for service in World War II. All of these images belong to the Municipal. Scattered in between are thousands of ordinary stories of ordinary lives—circuses, countless high school graduations, theatrical performances and the like, which filled the history of this place.

There could be no better setting for any ghost story than a dark and dimly lit morgue. In this regard, the Municipal does not disappoint. Walking through the cavernous basement of the Municipal Auditorium, the tone may easily conjure images of the old city morgue, with a coroner at work among the dead. The building reportedly functioned for a brief time as a temporary morgue for the city of Shreveport when Dr. Willis Butler served as coroner (see also the separate chapter on the ghost of Dr. Butler).[25] The basement still bears the evidence of this unique function, including the drains still visible in the floor, wall and floor tiles that could easily be cleaned and a separate ceiling and wall-mounted water and sprinkler system in the morgue area. All of these images from the past contribute to rich lore about the building and provide fodder for those who consistently report paranormal activity there.

The building's reputation has made it a desirable destination for a variety of paranormal and ghost-hunting organizations. Louisiana Spirits Paranormal Investigations was the first professional agency to investigate

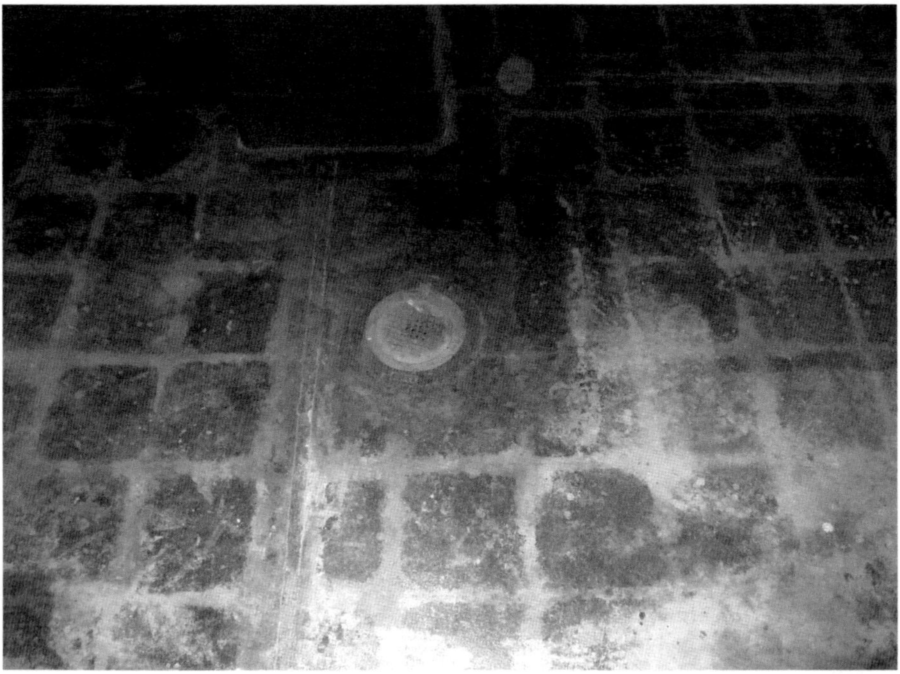

Drain in the floor in the basement of the Municipal Auditorium at the probable site of the temporary city morgue. *Photograph by Gary D. Joiner.*

reports of haunted activity at the Municipal Auditorium. Investigator Brandon Thomas became interested in the structure following reports of an apparition seen in one of the auditorium's main hallways, the sound of applause spontaneously erupting in a silent and vacant building and other strange and unexplained phenomena. The investigation yielded substantial data, leaving Thomas convinced that the building is haunted.

The Louisiana Spirits group recorded several electronic voice phenomena (EVP), as well as the registration of significant electromagnetic field (EMF) activity. The crew set up six infrared cameras inputting to an eight-channel DVR, with focuses on the stage, the floor of the auditorium, the ballroom and the basement. One was placed in the structure's main hallway where witnesses had reported seeing an apparition. The five investigators each carried a digital voice recorder and an electromagnetic field meter. Over several hours, the group gathered data from throughout the structure.[26]

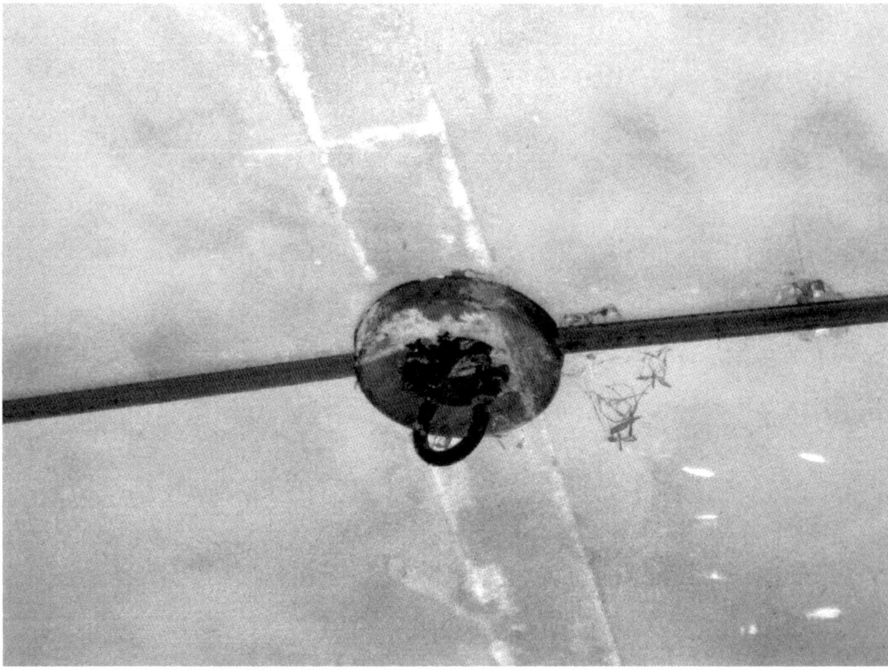

Ceiling assembly in the basement of Municipal Auditorium at the probable site of the temporary city morgue. *Photograph by Gary D. Joiner.*

Thomas reported there was a strong scent of flowers in one of the long-vacant dressing rooms. He heard the sound of chains being dropped on the floor while he and another team member were seated in the empty auditorium. In the area that once functioned as the city morgue, another investigator reported being pushed and scratched by an unseen presence. One of the crew members standing on the stage asked aloud for indication or proof of a spirit's presence and heard and recorded the distinct sound of clapping from directly in front of the stage. According to the published report of the Louisiana Spirits team, the audio evidence gathered during their investigation proved to be the most compelling. EVP recorded at the Municipal Auditorium, and now published on the website of the organization, include some that are quite clear and remarkable, such as a female voice saying, "I love Johnny Cash," and another that seems to be a person saying, "killed you." Another EVP voice says, "Get out of here."[27]

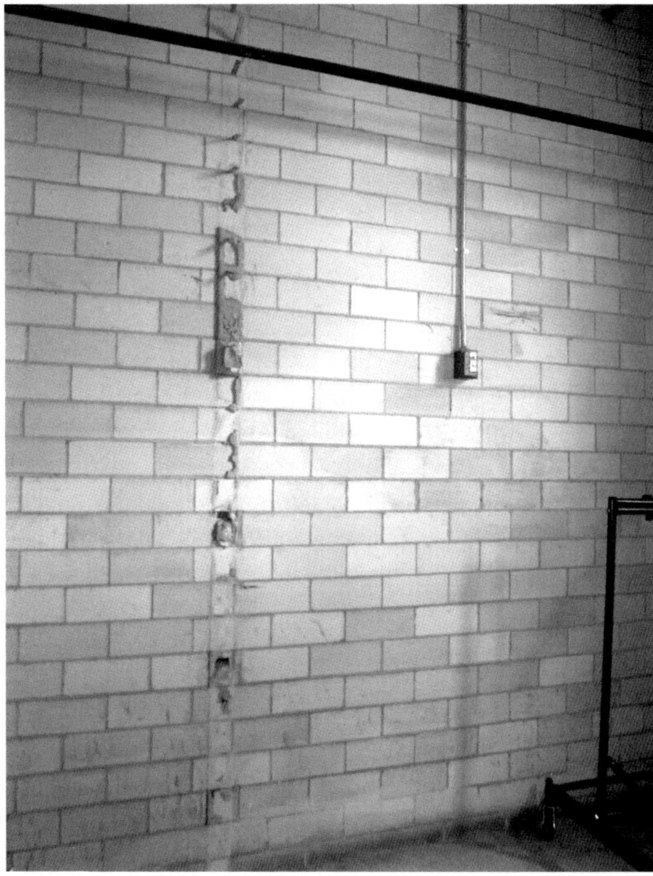

Wall showing the location of former water service and current electrical service in the basement of Municipal Auditorium at the probable site of the temporary city morgue. *Photograph by Gary D. Joiner.*

In October 2009, the Discovery Channel launched a new television series called *Ghost Lab* to explore unexplained supernatural phenomena at various locations throughout the country. The series featured two brothers, Brad and Barry Klinge, who depended on advanced technological means of investigating paranormal activity. With a personal history of having investigated over seventy separate paranormal sites, the brothers teamed up with the Discovery Channel to outfit a mobile "ghost lab," consisting of sophisticated audio, video and photographic equipment. The team's mobile laboratory boasted surveillance cameras with the ability to photograph from hundreds of feet away and in total darkness and also employed the use of thermal imaging technology. The first assignment for the *Ghost Lab* crew was the Municipal Auditorium in Shreveport, featured in the debut episode with a national and international audience on the Discovery Channel on October 6, 2009.[28]

What *Ghost Lab* investigators found as a result of their investigation of the Municipal Auditorium seems to parallel that of previous paranormal experts. They found a mysterious door that opened by itself on one of the upstairs balconies of the structure, and they recorded what they classified as a "Class A" EVP clearly audible without any digital enhancement. This voice seems to say, "They saw the light."[29]

The question of what conclusions might be drawn from the data gathered during these paranormal investigations must remain a subject of speculation, since there is no scientific proof that any of the observable activity was produced by a ghost at Municipal Auditorium. With the possible exception of the EVP recorded by Louisiana Spirits that seems to say, "I love Johnny Cash," and the recording of applause made by that same team of investigators, it is difficult to correlate the paranormal data collected with any particular aspect of the Municipal's history. The desire to ascribe the activity to the time when the Municipal Auditorium functioned as the stage for the *Louisiana Hayride* is easy to understand since this is, perhaps, the most easily romanticized era in the history of the structure. However, because the Municipal also functioned for a brief period of time as the morgue for the city of Shreveport, it is equally enticing to link the paranormal reports with that period as well. Perhaps the building has multiple ghosts that frequent its hallways, dressing rooms and basement.

History is what has kept the Municipal alive and, perhaps, saved it from the wrecking ball. By the last quarter of the twentieth century, the grand old structure was falling into decay and disrepair, but it was saved by the efforts of preservationists eager to retain this important marker of the city's past. Because of its significance to the historical and cultural identity of the city of Shreveport, state and local officials officially celebrated its designation as a National Historic Landmark in December 2009. The building previously was recognized by other agencies for its historical significance, but the "historic landmark" distinction carries greater import. It is the nation's highest designation for historic structures, reserved only for those buildings set aside by the United States

Department of the Interior because "they possess exceptional value or quality in illustrating or interpreting the heritage of the United States."[30] Not only will it likely encourage more rigorous attempts to maintain and preserve the structure, but it also means that funding for such efforts may be easier to obtain. It also places the Municipal Auditorium on a prestigious short list of historic sites across the entire United States that are recognized because they have meaning to all Americans.

The passing years have provided many opportunities for the Municipal Auditorium to become part of Shreveport's haunted history. Whether linked to its use as a city morgue or to its lively heyday of country music as home to the *Louisiana Hayride*, the haunted lore about this magnificent old building will continue to attract both curious visitors and paranormal investigators. Although the visitor may be drawn by the hope that the old walls will yield some measurable ghostly evidence of its past, the Municipal Auditorium will remain a beautiful but mostly silent witness. At their best, the ghostly tales associated with the Municipal Auditorium provide yet another means of telling the rich story of the city of Shreveport, its place in history and its significant contributions to the region, nation and world.

C.E. BYRD HIGH SCHOOL

To walk the halls of one of Shreveport's oldest public high schools is to risk an unexpected encounter with the supernatural, or so claim many of its faculty, students and visitors. They report frequent "cold spots," as well as unexplained lights and moaning noises from empty corridors. Some claim to hear the distant and mysterious echoes of a single gunshot. This ghost story has at least two different origins in local lore. One version has some basis in history, and the other is anecdotal. Variations of the much-repeated tale only contribute to the overall mystery. From one generation to the next, these stories assume new life, with an occasional twist or two of new insight. This interest is necessary, of course, to keep the legend alive. Consulting any Internet ghost-hunting site for north Louisiana, one finds pointed and frequent references to the haunting of C.E. Byrd High School. Any local who is educated on local ghost legends gives this school high paranormal attention. Yet again, history intersects the legends and gives these reports value while exploring a haunted chapter of Shreveport's past.

The first version of the story involves a young girl who allegedly drowned in the school's basement-level swimming pool during the earliest days of the school's operation. Historical inquiry yields no verification of this persistent legend or the girl's name. Further, the legend claims that the school officials filled in the swimming pool and the ghost of the girl haunts that area of the school even today. It is true that the high school, when first opened, boasted an indoor Olympic-size swimming pool, but there is no verifiable record of a drowning there. In 1937, the school built a new gymnasium on top of the area that housed the swimming pool.[31] Another version of haunting competes with the drowning story to explain the unusual activity at Byrd High School. In October 1962, an ROTC instructor, cleaning rifles before school one morning, discharged a loaded weapon and killed himself. Again, this reportedly took place in the basement of the school. One variation claims that the incident was suicide, but again, historical examination does not reach that conclusion. Local media reports document the event. Police and coroner's inquest reports determined that the shooting was accidental. As is often the case in ghost stories, however, the facts must compete heavily with more popular folklore weaved through decades of retelling.

Yet again, a historian finds the unique promise of folklore to provide a window into the true history of the era in Shreveport history, its influences, personalities and developments. In this case, these haunted tales provide an interesting opportunity to look back through the lens of history and discover more about a school that has always been a veritable fortress of Shreveport identity. To understand the culture that has produced such persistent haunted lore, it is necessary to understand that C.E. Byrd High School in Shreveport is collective legend itself. The school has contributed so much to Shreveport history and identity that it has earned its nickname of "the City of Byrd." From its beginnings in 1925, the school has been the educational home for many of the region's most influential movers and shakers, and each new incoming freshman class continues to renew its place in the city's rich culture.

The school is a massive structure, a product of the same exciting and exuberant decade that produced the city's Municipal Auditorium as well as the current Caddo Parish Courthouse. These buildings share in common reports as haunted places. They also occupy a unique shared space within Shreveport history, during a period of hopeful anticipation in the aftermath of the Great War, and the architecture of the period

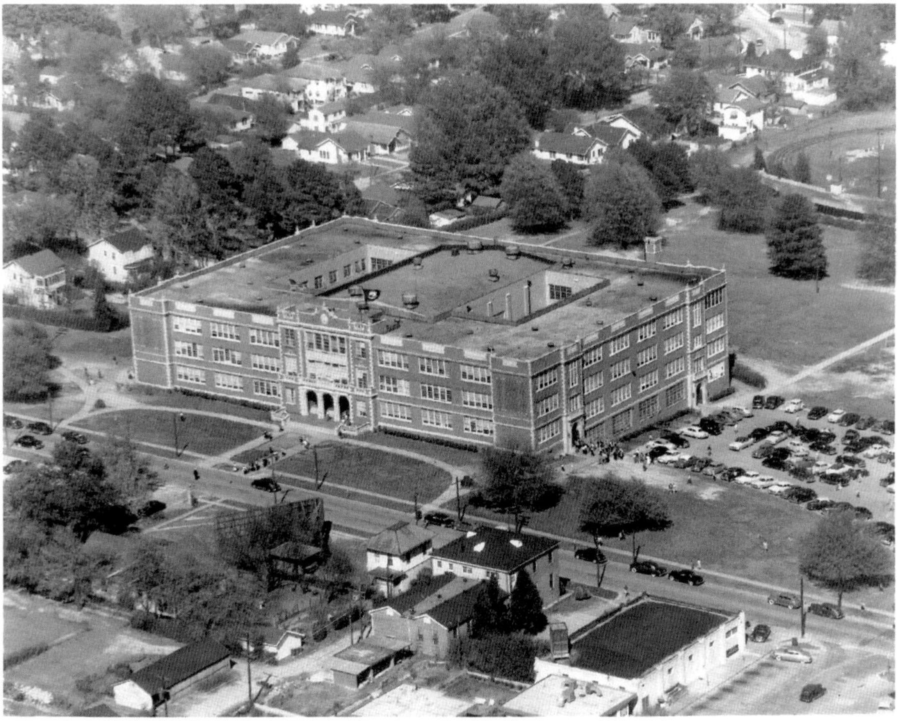

Aerial view of C.E. Byrd High School in the 1950s. *Courtesy of Archives and Special Collections, Louisiana State University in Shreveport.*

certainly expressed this attitude. Shreveport was a place of building and prosperity, basking in the reputation as the oil capital of the area. The C.E. Byrd High School building was constructed during a period of transition in the early part of the century. Changing social attitudes began to embrace such new concepts and question old ones, as evidenced by women's suffrage, civil rights and expanded public education.

In this environment, C.E. Byrd High School became a reality, but it owes its origins to the overall change in how children were educated in 1925. Louisiana did not generally view education as a priority—a commonly held view in the South following the Civil War—and the city of Shreveport was a fair mirror of that attitude even as the new century approached. Many citizens and officials still viewed public education as something for the poor who could not afford private instruction. Only the most liberal of policymakers had such a vision.

Much of the public attitude that slowed educational progress stemmed from inherited ideas that education was needed only in the realm of basic subjects. With a primarily agrarian economy, the South suffered from a cultural disparity that minimized the need for education in a primarily agrarian economy. Before the outbreak of Civil War, many areas in the North had already provided for tax-supported public school facilities, while the South was only beginning to consider this concept.[32]

As early as 1888, the Louisiana legislature acted to allow high schools to be built across the state, but this legislation left much of the budgetary concerns over such construction and maintenance to local municipalities that wanted the schools. The local school board made repeated requests for funding in the late nineteenth century, but requests were repeatedly denied. This led to a lawsuit against the Shreveport City Council, with many area progressives leading the charge for proper allocation of funds from poll taxes to benefit education.[33]

C.E. Byrd High School was not the first Shreveport school for secondary education. The first public high school operated within the Young Men's Christian Association (YMCA) in downtown Shreveport. Also home to the local chapter of the Salvation Army, Shreveport's first high school opened its doors to a mere forty students in 1892. Clifton Ellis (C.E.) Byrd served as the principal. Like other schools of the era, the standards of study were strict, with a heavy emphasis on the liberal arts.[34] Byrd was a Virginia native, born in 1868 and trained as a lawyer at the University of Virginia before he entered the educational field.[35]

It did not take long for conditions at the new school to become congested, with enrollments swelling by the next year. The school board was at least partially prepared for such expansion, with the purchase of land on Hope Street in Shreveport. However, construction delays resulted from the local effects of a generalized national economic downturn on the local economy, and advocates of secondary education turned to private donors for assistance.[36]

By 1899, local school officials celebrated the opening of Shreveport Central High School, popularly called Hope Street School. The massive three-story structure housed primary and secondary grades and represented the best in modern construction. Professor Byrd was concerned about the lack of access to a quality library, so when noted philanthropist Andrew Carnegie offered to assist with a new library for the city, Byrd pressed for the school to be its location. However, funding failed when area voters declined Carnegie's offer, and, again, the school turned to private contributors.[37] Shreveport Central High School, in the spirit of Professor C.E. Byrd, projected a self-reliant determination to provide quality education, which was still an uncommon understanding of public education in many parts of the South at this time.

Throughout the first three decades of the twentieth century, the city's population continued to expand at significant rates. By 1920, local voters were more than willing to support the construction of a new school. This facility was located next to Central School, which assumed the role of primary education. The new building allowed for the segregation of the lower grades from the high school by housing them in the new building. The first annual yearbook of the new school accurately reflected the source of economic prosperity for the region. Simply called the *Gusher*, it captured the great spirit of optimism so closely linked to the recent booming production in large oil fields of the region.[38]

Shreveport history during the first decades of the twentieth century has roots in the oil boom and the unexpected infusion of economic prosperity in an agrarian economy. This found expression in many public institutions of the period, including the public schools. In the summer of 1901, near Jennings, Louisiana, the discovery of a major oil field made national news, and it had regional impact.[39] Before long, the oil and gas industry claimed the center stage of Louisiana's economic interests, and many people pinned their personal and community hopes on the promise of this rich natural resource. This attitude was certainly prevalent in Shreveport in the booming new century, so citizens found new sources of unexpected wealth.

The coming of World War I also shaped this period in Shreveport history as citizens responded to the patriotic call of their nation at war. Shreveport public schools participated in conservation efforts for commodities needed for the war. This dramatic national backdrop, coupled with the regional excitement over newfound prosperity, had profound impact on Shreveport's embrace of progress and hopes for the future.

The period also demonstrates the timelessness of key controversies that plague public education. As the second decade of the twentieth century dawned in Shreveport, public education witnessed a conflict over prayer in schools. Professor Byrd believed that the practice of prayer in a public school setting was unconstitutional, but pressure brought by many local organizations and individuals forced him to accept the practice. However, the case of *Herold et al vs. Caddo Parish School Board* confirmed Byrd's belief and strongly affirmed separation of church and state.[40] Sidney Herold, a local Jewish attorney and former Louisiana constitutional convention delegate, made a career of pressing the issue of church and state through challenges in the justice system. This 1915 lawsuit in the Louisiana Supreme Court became the precedent and basis for a later United States Supreme Court ruling on the same issue.[41] Shreveport public education had actually been at the center of a lively national constitutional debate, shaping the forces of history on this controversial issue.

More progress toward the construction of what would become C.E. Byrd High School as a separate institution of public learning took place in the early 1920s. A special committee of the school board selected the present site on Line Avenue for a new facility. The ceremony placing the building's cornerstone was held in October 1924, and Shreveport was on its way to the building of a new place of legends. Professor Byrd himself performed the honors that day and immediately departed to seek treatment for advancing tuberculosis. Just one year later, the new school named in his honor became reality when the doors officially opened to the next generation of students. "My reward is sure," Byrd noted in his dedication ceremony address. He died just a few months later.[42] Through the school that continues to bear his name, his reputation as the father of Caddo's public schools lives on.

The march of time brought changes to the high school as new generations passed through its massive front doors. Leaving the school each year were many who became important civic and business leaders, and its reputation grew to embrace the idea of the "City of Byrd." When built, Byrd High School sat in a remote area of town, not much developed in the residential sense. That situation resolved itself as the city expanded to the south and families moved to the suburbs, making enrollments grow. The City of Byrd witnessed the decade of despair, the 1930s and the Great Depression, as none in that era could have been unaffected by these dramatic events in history. But with the coming of the Second World War, the school gave much to history as young male graduates left to enlist. A significant development in the school's curriculum during the 1930s was the introduction of the elective class of ROTC—the Reserve Officer Training Corps.[43]

The decade of the 1930s may have been the origin of one of Byrd's persistent ghost stories, that of the young girl who haunts the gymnasium built atop what was originally the swimming pool of the original structure. In 1937, the school filled in the pool to build the foundation for the gym. Though the historical record cannot document the events related in the ghost tale, the sealing of the pool and construction of the gym, a burial of sorts, may have helped to cement its popular urban legend. A survey of haunted folklore common to areas across the United States produces the predictable conclusion that death by drowning is a popular generator of ghosts.[44] How or why this particular ghost story began is anyone's guess, but it is proof of the long-term survivability of this type of lore.

Byrd High School was a representative microcosm of every major historical signpost of the twentieth century. The fact that the school produced no annual yearbook for the war years of 1943, 1944 and 1945 only serves to underscore this assertion, as students and faculty tried to do their part to conserve paper, a needed commodity of war.[45] The football rivalry of Byrd High School and another Shreveport high school, Fair Park, always drew huge and enthusiastic crowds in an annual display of school pride on the gridiron. However, the 1942 match-up reported the worst turnout in either school's history.[46]

The school continued to reflect national trends as the population of the city expanded dramatically in the first "baby boom" years of the late 1940s and 1950s. This ushered in "the Golden Age of Byrd," when the school dominated in athletics and academics. The school had a well-established reputation of excellence that found expression in new social concerns, including a topic of campus discussion on "What Would You Do If an Atomic Bomb Fell Near You?"[47]

Future decades brought new challenges; an important one of the 1970s was the issue of school desegregation. The local plan ("the crossover") merged black and white schools through an exchange of both students and teachers from the traditionally black Valencia High School (now the site of Caddo Magnet High School) with the white population of Byrd High School. Tensions ran high in the spring of 1970 as both races had to adjust to unfamiliar social and cultural circumstances. It was a time marked by uncertainty and a good deal of disagreement about the relative success of the desegregation movement. In 1977, the U.S. Justice Department announced that Caddo Parish still had too many racially segregated schools, so the school board had to undertake further measures to ensure compliance with federal mandates.[48] By the end of that decade, Byrd High School had survived the test of desegregation, but both attendance and enrollment declined, and the physical plant fell into disrepair. LSU Shreveport's professor emeritus of history, Dr. Ann McLaurin, accurately described it this way: "The old Byrd building had survived three wars, the Great Depression and revolutionary social changes, but paint was peeling from the ceilings and plaster was falling from the walls."[49]

The school underwent great renovation and revival in the decades that followed, particularly throughout the 1980s. The tragic death of an ROTC instructor rocked the foundations of the Byrd High School community in 1962. This is the origin of the second popular ghost legends about the school. Although persistent repeating of the legend indicates that the instructor, an experienced marksman, master sergeant and war veteran, committed suicide in the school's firing range, there is no historical evidence to verify this claim. The police reports about the shooting, as well as the coroner's report submitted by Dr. Willis Butler, indicate that the official cause of death was ruled as accidental.[50] It would seem that the ROTC instructor made the fatal and careless assumption that the chamber of his rifle was empty when he peered down the bore during routine cleaning of the weapon. Since that day at Byrd High School, many reports have been made of a single eerie and unexplained gunshot echoing throughout the hallways of the school. By the 1990s, the ROTC program at Byrd High School had the distinction of having the largest enrollment in any such program in the nation. Furthermore, the program has repeatedly received the highest designation awarded by the United States Army.[51]

Apart from the allure of a good ghost story in a massive old building that echoes with the voices of the past, the story of C.E. Byrd High School provides a relevant and meaningful snapshot of Shreveport's past. The school has produced a long list of distinguished alumni who not only contributed significantly to the city's development and history but also some whose ambitions took them to state and national service. Distinguished graduates include such people as John Dalton, secretary of the United States Navy during the Clinton administration (1993–1998); J. Bennett Johnston, former United States senator from Louisiana; as well as countless other civic and business leaders who have done much to shape local and regional history. Its immovable place in the development of city culture secures the place of Byrd High School in the story of Shreveport. The ghosts of Byrd High School, whoever they may be, haunt a beautiful old place intertwined with the drama that is Shreveport history.

DR. WILLIS BUTLER

Dr. Willis P. Butler is perhaps the longest-serving public official in Shreveport history, and still serving! Late-night sightings of Dr. Willis P. Butler, long-serving medical examiner and coroner of Caddo Parish, are common in some areas of the local courthouse and other buildings in downtown Shreveport. More than one government employee has nodded to speak to the former coroner or noticed his passing presence in a room. There is nothing particularly odd or unusual about noting the presence of a public servant in a government building at any time of the day. But Dr. Willis Butler has been dead since 1991. By all accounts, he is a kind spirit, quietly going about his work, apparently not wishing to disturb others. If this is true, in death he is much as he was in life.

Butler's long and productive medical career spanned decades of service as coroner and medical examiner, but his interests reached far beyond autopsies and inquests. He was also interested in helping the living, and this marked him as a true pioneer in the treatment of drug addiction. His death at the age of 103 seemed to end a distinguished medical career, yet there are indications that Dr. Butler appears at his work site still, at least occasionally. There are no unexplained occurrences, odd events, strange noises or ghostly apparitions to speak of in this haunting, only the unthreatening and professional presence of a man who dedicated his entire life to the service of his community.

This ghost story lacks the popular and sensationalized appeal of others chronicled in Shreveport's history. Those unfamiliar with Dr. Butler's remarkable contributions to history and his important medical legacy might not seek out his ghost, or if they dared, they might not know exactly where to look. Furthermore, he seems to have limited his appearances to the areas of Shreveport where he spent much of his work life, including those that are still in use for public service and are accessed by hundreds of people each day for routine business. The story of Dr. Butler's ghost does not draw the curiosity seekers to old buildings that speak only of the past. Instead, his is a ghost story that is told within the framework of an ever-changing and dynamic public history. The proper telling of this story does not involve mere haunted structures or sites; rather, it relates to the life of a remarkable man whose life bridged two centuries in Shreveport history.

To know Dr. Butler is to understand the meaning of hard work and dedication to the calling of a physician. He was a principled man who responded to the needs of his community in many different ways, whether it was in his official capacity as medical examiner or as a visionary clinician intent on addressing one of the early twentieth century's most challenging social ills. The passion with which he lived his life is perhaps the energy that lives on now, roaming surroundings in downtown Shreveport that were familiar to him. A ghost might not be simply a dead human being who roams an earthly dimension. Another common explanation, even among skeptics, is that a ghost is simply a manifestation of personal energy that remains behind, imprinted on the structures and places that had been important in life. By this definition, Dr. Butler is certainly a ghost of the courthouse.

The current Caddo Parish Courthouse, built in 1926, stands on the site of two previous structures dating to the city's early history. With its geography at the center of the downtown area, the building and its site have doubtlessly witnessed much in the passage of Shreveport history. The first courthouse actually served briefly as the capital of the Confederate state of Louisiana during the Civil War, until advancing Union troops prompted government officials to hastily relocate operations to the northern part of the state. The

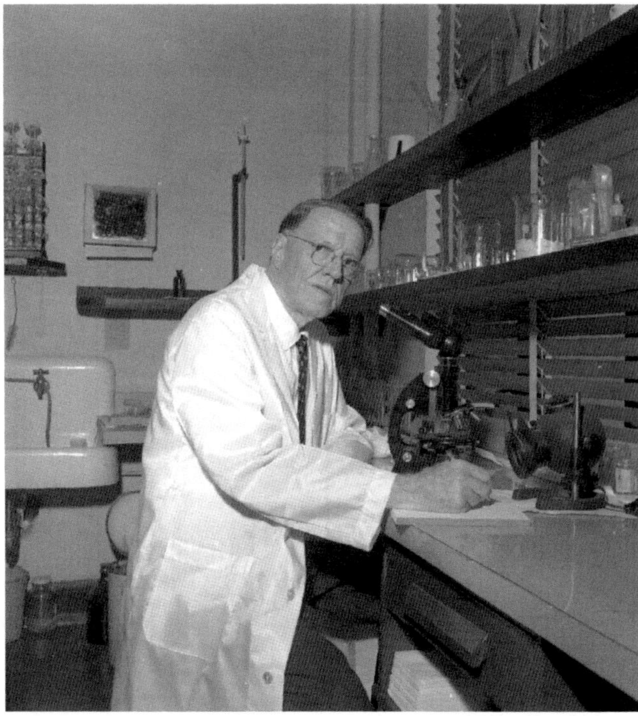

Dr. Willis Butler in his laboratory. *Courtesy of Archives and Special Collections, Louisiana State University in Shreveport.*

current structure has been the site of the execution of many criminals, by the eighth-floor gallows or by Louisiana's traveling electric chair. If ever a building were haunted, the courthouse would be a likely contender. Due to its past, the courthouse has been the subject of local ghost legends and lore. Some government officials say, without qualification, that it is haunted. They have seen Dr. Butler. Witnesses have reported sightings in the basement of the courthouse and particularly on the building's fourth floor.

The fourth floor of the Caddo Parish Courthouse was the site of a gruesome murder/attempted suicide during Butler's tenure as coroner. In his own book, *Will Somebody Call the Coroner?*, Dr. Butler described the event from the perspective of his position as the coroner and that of a witness of sorts, since he heard the shots fired that day through his open courthouse office window. The shooting occurred in the office of the city engineer. A disgruntled employee fired at the city engineer and then turned the pistol on himself in an unsuccessful suicide attempt.[52] This event has all the ingredients of a ghost story in its own right, even without the added interest of the attending coroner nearby. Witnesses have also reported seeing Dr. Butler in and around the Municipal Auditorium, further advancing the legend that a portion of that structure within the basement once served temporarily as the city morgue. Although some dispute this, it remains a popular aspect of local folklore, and evidence in the basement of the building seems to support such an argument. Dr. Butler's ghostly presence there can neither substantiate nor refute the claim, but it is an interesting association. Additionally, for a period in the early twentieth century, the Shreveport Sanitarium occupied a city block on the corner of Grand and Texas Avenues, just down the street from the site of the Municipal Auditorium. Therefore, it is likely that Dr. Butler frequented both of these locations in the conduct of his daily business.

Born in Gibsland, Louisiana, in 1888, Willis Butler moved with family to Shreveport in 1899 and graduated from Shreveport Central High School in 1907. From there he went to study medicine at Vanderbilt University.[53] It was a time in the history of medicine when research, discovery and everyday general practice all seemed the same. Rapid advances in understanding of diseases and their treatments completely transformed the role of the physician. Willis Butler entered the practice of medicine at a time in history when his talents were appreciated. He brought with him an inquiring and open mind, committed to seeking meaningful cures and not mere palliation. His natural and boundless curiosity drove him to investigate, question and publish conclusions, even if they at times seemed controversial. His life path brought him back to Shreveport following his medical training. He served the community for decades, most notably as coroner of Caddo Parish from 1916 to 1961 and again from 1973 to 1976.

Butler married Annie Perry Dodd in 1913. Their alliance originated during Annie's frequent trips to Shreveport to visit her brother, Monroe Dodd, the pastor of First Baptist Church. When Butler became coroner in 1916, he initiated a long term of service that witnessed important milestones in death investigations, including the use of photographs as evidence.[54] Many years of public service made Dr. Butler prominent among the citizenry of Shreveport and cemented his ties to the community.

Dr. Butler was so respected that city officials sided with him in one of the most controversial aspects of his tenure as Caddo Parish coroner—and the unwavering support of Shreveport officials probably saved him from federal indictment in 1923.[55] Perhaps his most visionary service came from the establishment of a drug treatment clinic that he operated from 1919 to 1923. It was first located at Shreveport's Charity Hospital, then the City Jail and finally at a house on McNeil Street in downtown Shreveport. The clinic's purpose was to treat those addicted to morphine by close supervision and decreasing dosages of the narcotic. The city's large number of morphine addicts alarmed Dr. Butler and moved him to address the problem in a meaningful and enlightened way. Dr. Butler believed that the city's morphine addiction rate was high because of two factors: incurable illnesses (e.g., cancer) and chronic pain brought on by years of manual labor.[56]

Dr. Butler's revolutionary approach to treating morphine addicts as if they had a treatable illness was a notion well ahead of its time. At a time in history when medical practitioners routinely believed drug addiction to be a matter of personal weakness or lack of restraint, Dr. Butler believed that no one desired such a state for himself. At this time the criminal justice system, though not the medical field, routinely dealt with drug addiction through the simple remedy of incarceration. As an alternative, and through a professional and discreet clinical setting in downtown Shreveport, Dr. Butler quietly but aggressively sought a cure for the morphine addict. He purchased morphine in wholesale lots and then sold it to patients at a small profit—just enough to cover the clinic's operations. By allowing patients to come in to register for treatment under assumed names, Dr. Butler helped to alleviate the social stigma associated with addiction.[57] The nation's drug addiction rate at the turn of the twentieth century must have been alarming, but it was a natural byproduct of the standard medical treatment protocols of the preceding decades.

At this time in United States history the use of opium products was undergoing an interesting cultural change, and society found increasing challenges in dealing with its implications. During the nineteenth century, opiates had been routinely used as home remedies for many types of physical ailments. Throughout America, opium was a staple product readily available in a variety of commercial and retail settings. It was common for general storekeepers to function as local pharmacists, despite a lack of training or true clinical understanding of the drug's potency.[58]

Nineteenth-century medicine included the use of drugs with powerful properties (such as opium) and bleeding of patients as the mainstays of the general practitioner. Over the course of the century, the popularity of opiates increased, and attempts to regulate the powerful drugs did not exist before 1858. In that year, the American Pharmaceutical Association declared its intent to begin restricting drug dispensing by physicians and other practitioners. By then, opium was as common a prescription as over-the-counter pain relievers are in the modern society. The wide range of medicinal uses for these drugs supported this practice.[59]

Physicians first identified morphine as the major derivative of opium in the late nineteenth century. This new compound appeared to be a milder prescriptive alternative to opium itself. At the same time, significant advances arose in the use of hypodermics. As a result, injected morphine became the new treatment for a variety of ills. Yet another pharmaceutical development came on the heels of morphine, one that continues to the present day. Heroin first came into use at the turn of the twentieth century, promoted by the Bayer Company. Clinicians of the day viewed it as a safer drug than morphine.[60] The widespread and enthusiastic use of these highly addictive substances in common medical practice contributed to a significant population of drug addicts in the early twentieth century.

As an urban center, Shreveport was not immune to these social ills in the period following World War I. The medical practices of the preceding century created an American drug problem, and Dr. Butler believed that medical practice held the key to its solution. He was one of a pioneering few in American medical history who saw a biochemical cause for addiction, one that clinicians could treat with gradually reducing dosages so as not to induce a state of withdrawal in the patient. Dr. Butler believed that it was a physical need, not an emotional weakness, that drove the addict to seek continual doses of morphine. This belief was shared by others, and Dr. Butler was able to obtain a license for his clinic to operate in the state of Louisiana. Other clinics using this approach at the same time were found in New York and Jacksonville, Florida. The clinics shared a common medical understanding of morphine addiction based on the concepts of physical tolerance and withdrawal.[61]

In March 1921, the Louisiana State Board of Health discontinued its supervision of Butler's clinic, citing compliance with the 1914 Harrison Act, a federal law that controlled the distribution of morphine and other opiates. Like the Volstead Act and Eighteenth Amendment to the Constitution that prohibited the manufacture, distribution and sale of alcoholic beverages, the Harrison Act was part of politically progressive attempts to realign society along common moral themes. While the Harrison Act broadly allowed physicians to continue to use opiate drugs for their recognized medical uses (pain relief), the act was, at its core, a revenue measure of the federal government aimed at taxing unlicensed sellers of the drug. For this reason, individual practitioners did not immediately feel the enforcement of the act's provisions, especially since the law's constitutionality derived primarily from its revenue function. The United States Supreme Court decided in 1916 that physicians could maintain addicts through medical supervision.[62] However, increasing federal bureaucracy aimed at enforcing the measure eventually meant oversight of the drug's proper medical usages.[63] In 1919, the court reversed its decision of three years earlier, making it a federal offense for any physician to continue with medical maintenance of drug addicts.[64] Yet the day after Butler's clinic lost its oversight from the Louisiana State Board of Health, the City of Shreveport unanimously passed an ordinance permitting his work with his addicted patients to continue. "It would be criminal to have abruptly discontinued their care," Butler wrote following the city's decision.[65]

The City of Shreveport's decision to allow Butler to operate in violation of federal law stands as strong testimony to the esteem the physician enjoyed. It also speaks to the rate of success in treatment. In one of several peer-reviewed medical journals in which he recounted his success, Butler cited that the clinic population in Shreveport dropped from 740 addicts to 120 addicts during the four years of operation.[66] When writing for peers in the medical community, Butler was unafraid to reveal the depth of his compassion for the addicts he was helping: "No matter what different persons may call the condition, the patient is a sick person and as such is entitled to and should have proper considerations, care and treatment—either for the causes that are responsible for him being an addict or the addiction itself."[67]

By 1923, the federal government began applying pressure on Caddo District Attorney Philip Mecom to shut down Butler's clinic. Under the threat of indictments for public officials, including the coroner, the City of Shreveport yielded to federal law.[68] Nevertheless, Dr. Butler's treatment plan became an exemplary model for future generations of medical practitioners interested in the disease concept of addiction. His pioneering work rapidly advanced the cause of drug abuse treatment to nurturing modern applications. To the end of his life, Dr. Butler always recounted this aspect of his career with particular pride.

Abounding energy and quiet professionalism marked Dr. Butler's numerous years of public service to the people of Shreveport and Caddo Parish. For decades, he was a prominent and well-respected part of civic life and a sought-after forensics and medical witness (even in his later years) thanks to the diversity of his expertise. During his career, he witnessed much in the advance of forensic medicine and the changing role of the parish coroner. For instance, he was among the first to use photographs for crime scene reconstruction.[69]

Dr. Butler's natural curiosity seemed to know no limits, and neither did his courage. His 1991 obituary recounted a famous anecdote. It indicated that "he once strapped on his pistol, traveled out in the parish in a horse and buggy, picked up both the victim's body and the suspected killer."[70] Dr. Butler himself recounted a similar tale of driving twenty-six miles from Hosston, Louisiana, back to Shreveport with an accused murderer in the car with him—wrists tied to the car door. On the way, a tire blew out on his car, and he changed the tire on a rural road with the prisoner still tied inside. "Never again did I go alone on a murder case," Butler reported.[71] Stories like this characterized the life of a fascinating man.

It is fitting that Dr. Butler would continue to visit places in Shreveport that witnessed so much of his life's work: the Caddo Parish Courthouse, the streets of downtown Shreveport that he doubtless walked every day, perhaps even the Municipal Auditorium. All of these places were his professional homes. It is easy to imagine him at work in those places even today, if only in spirit. If physical buildings can truly bear the imprint of personalities, then it is plausible that the ghost of this remarkable public servant indeed haunts these sites.

THE LOGAN MANSION

The Logan Mansion at 725 Austin Place (originally known as Christian Street) is an example of the Victorian/Queen Anne architecture that once dominated home design at the end of the nineteenth century. Noted architect Nathaniel Sykes Allen designed and built the home in 1897. The structure has stood in a historic area of Shreveport for 113 years, and in many ways, it is typical of houses in historic and architectural districts across America. The story of the home echoes those of impressive old structures. It begins with its function as a residence, then as home to various commercial establishments before it fell into disrepair and neglect. Unlike some less fortunate old homes, the Logan Mansion has returned to its original purpose as a private residence. It is haunted, if not by "real" ghosts, then certainly by the ghosts of a bygone era of Shreveport's grandeur.

Today, the present owners of the seventeen-room mansion, Bill and Vicki LeBrun, are restoring it to its original splendor. They have enthusiastically accepted the challenge of this grand old home of Shreveport that is also one of the few remaining intact and original structures in one of the city's most elite turn-of-the-century neighborhoods. The home has also been the source of some of the most persistent haunted and ghostly lore in the city's history. Its stories include many of the stereotypical elements expected in the genre, those of tragic early death and a soul unwilling to move on from this earthly existence.

The moniker "Logan Mansion" continues to describe the structure today, respecting the memory of the home's original builders and owners, Lafayette Robert Logan and his wife, Lavinia "Livie" Wilson Logan. Although the home has changed ownership numerous times in the past century, it has never relinquished its name, even when it served as a commercial structure. The patriarch of the mansion, Robert Logan, was born in Virginia in November 1848 and served as a colonel in the Confederate army before moving even farther south following the war.[72] As is common in Shreveport history, the story of the Logans speaks to the economic potential that many must have perceived in the new city on the Red River. The couple married in 1896, one year before the mansion was completed.[73] They built their mansion in what was known as the Hicks Subdivision, spanning thirty city blocks, and now a prized historic district.

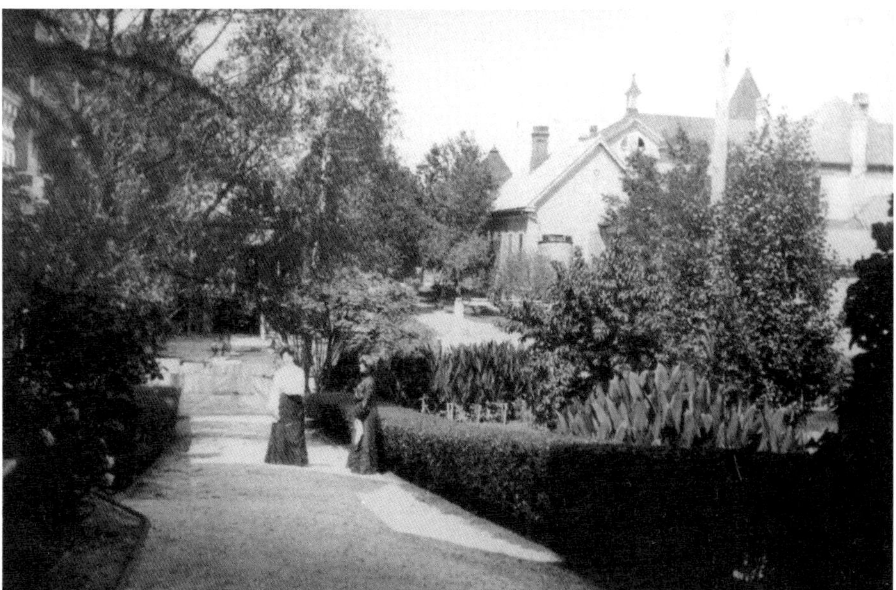

Undated photograph of Livinia "Livie" Logan and Nina Seay Logan in the gardens of the Logan Mansion. *Courtesy of Archives and Special Collections, Louisiana State University in Shreveport.*

Eventually, the area came to encompass surrounding neighborhoods near the downtown area, including the historic Ledbetter Heights, home to the city's once-thriving and infamous red-light district. Operating from 1903 to 1917, this legal prostitution district also promoted the arts with noted musicians such as Huddie William Ledbetter, also known as "Leadbelly," who contributed so much to the cultural fabric of the city that the area bears his name. The nearby high ground in this area near downtown Shreveport, Allendale, attracted the wealthy to build homes there.

Near the Logan Mansion are two other notable haunted locations for the curious tourist, both within easy walking distance. Just down the street is one of the entrances to Oakland Cemetery, the eternal resting place of many of Shreveport's most influential early settlers. Around the corner and across the street from the Oakland Cemetery is the Municipal Auditorium, built in the 1920s and one of the most haunted places in all of the southern United States, continually attracting ghost hunters and paranormal investigators from all over the nation. This area is fascinating not only because of its historic relevance to the city but also because it continues to have places that attract new interest and others that are left to decay. Oakland Cemetery, Logan Mansion and the Municipal Auditorium are high points in historic preservation. This area represents a complex crossroads of past and present and speaks a strong message about the importance of inner city revitalization and renewal.

This Shreveport neighborhood was the home of the elite at the turn of the twentieth century and mirrored the social and familial trends of the age. Census records show that the Logan Mansion was home to an extended family, including Livie's mother, brother and sister-in-law.[74] While tradition was that the Logan fortune came from beer distribution, the 1900 census indicated Robert Logan's occupation as "ice manufacturer."[75] Indeed, Logan did both. His company was the Shreveport Ice and Brewery Company.[76] Evidence of the family ties to a vocation involving beer is prominently and permanently displayed at the home. Carvings of hops used in the manufacture of beer are seen in the massive pinewood trim of the home's great rooms. The Logans were buried in the city's historic Oakland Cemetery, just down the street. During the winter, their grand old home is visible from their graves.

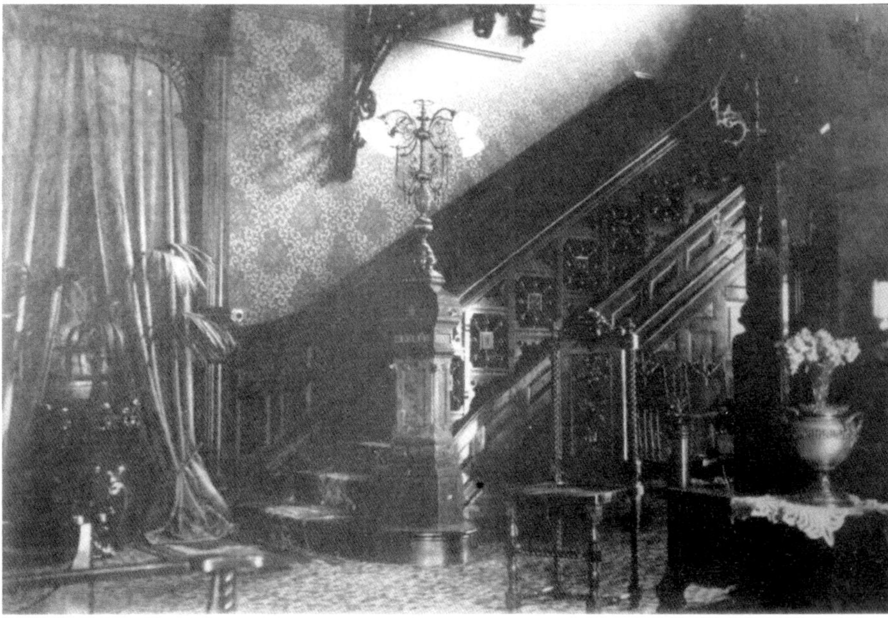

Period photograph of the foyer of the Logan Mansion. *Courtesy of Archives and Special Collections, Louisiana State University in Shreveport.*

Booming prosperity marked the period of Shreveport in which the Logans lived. This is typical of other American cities during the Gilded Age. During this era, the city enjoyed substantial growth in population as its economy and social health recovered from the devastating yellow fever epidemic of 1873 that claimed hundreds of lives and disrupted civic life. In addition, Shreveport benefited from its position as a crossroads of trade and commerce, attracting wealth to the ranks of the already established population. As national manufacturing production grew at exponential rates, it provided commercial traffic to destinations throughout the South and Southwest, Shreveport among them. Much like other cities across the country, Shreveport's citizenry reflected the same extravagant displays of excess that resulted from an influx of industrial and commercial wealth. The Logan Mansion is an example and reminder of all the opulence and grandeur that was part of Shreveport's Gilded Age. It was one of many homes built on Austin Place that characterized residential preferences of this new business/merchant class.

The turn of the twentieth century in Shreveport history brought rapid changes as the city began to expand to the west and south. The Logan home's history is both interesting and tragic. Intersecting the story of the Gilded Age commercial magnate Robert Logan is that of a Shreveport physician, Dr. Randall Hunt, and his wife, Emily. The Hunts lived in a neighboring home across the street from the Logans in the first decade of the new twentieth century. Dr. Hunt was born in 1866 in East Feliciana Parish in Louisiana to farmer parents. He studied at Tulane University Medical School[77] and, in Shreveport, worked to help establish the Shreveport Charity Hospital (later known as Confederate Memorial Hospital and today Louisiana State University Health Sciences Center). Randall Hunt and his wife were parents to four children at the time they lived as neighbors to the Logans.[78] According to traditional lore, one of the Hunts' daughters, Theodora, jumped from the third-floor attic

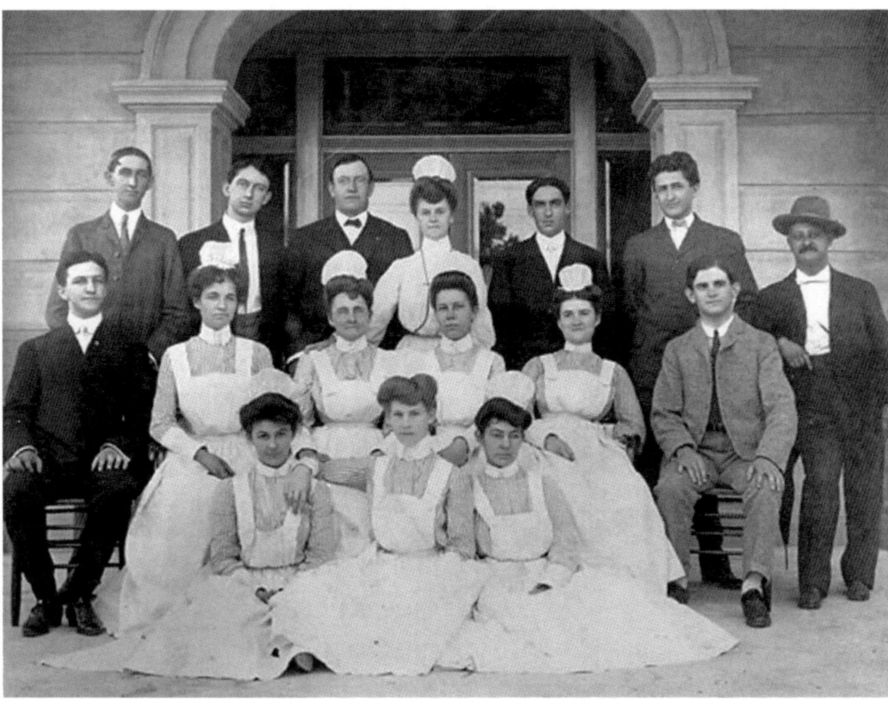

Group photograph of Dr. Randall Hunt (top row, third from left) and the medical and nursing staff of Shreveport Charity Hospital. *Courtesy of Louisiana State University Health Sciences Center.*

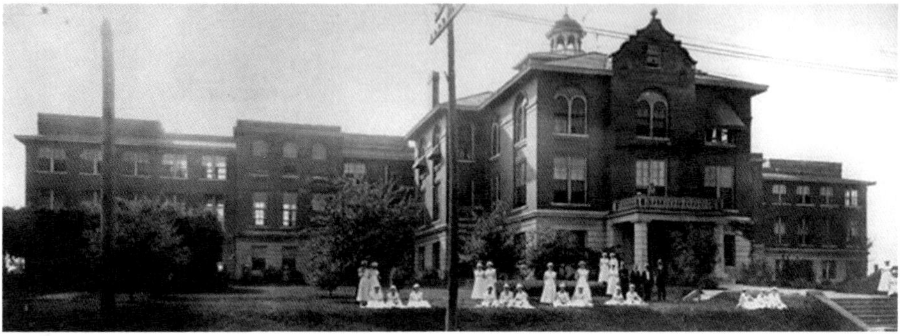

Shreveport Charity Hospital at the turn of the twentieth century. *Courtesy of Louisiana State University Health Sciences Center.*

window of the Logan home and suffered what would prove to be fatal injuries. Many legends surrounding the incident portray a troubled young girl, perhaps even mentally unstable, who jumped to commit suicide.

This tragedy has served as the explanation for the Logan Mansion's long history of strange events and paranormal activity, but it has also raised questions about what might have attracted Theodora to the Logan home since the Logans had no children of their own. Considering the extended family living at the Logan Mansion in 1900, it is possible that the Logan in-laws had small children who may have been playmates of the Hunt children. Upon the death of the Logans, the Wade Hampton family purchased the home. Following Mr. Hampton's retirement from Kansas City Southern Railway, the home became a boardinghouse.[79] According to tradition, the Hamptons converted the mansion's massive attic into rented space for teachers. It seems that the earliest legendary accounts of strange activity in the home may date to this period of its history. One of the alternative versions of the Theodora Hunt story involves the mysterious death of a six- to eight-year-old girl who was said to be the daughter of a teacher who rented space in the boardinghouse.

Following its use as a boardinghouse, the Logan Mansion became a base for various church and community organizations. Later, in the 1970s, historic preservationists voiced concerns about maintaining the integrity of the structure as the neighborhood rapidly declined. At this time, preservationists were concerned that many of the remaining grand homes of the Austin Place area were being demolished or were in serious states of decay and disrepair. Shreveport faced the real possibility of losing another visible link to this opulent era in history.

In 1976, the Shreveport Broadcasting Company purchased the Logan Mansion and converted its rooms for use as a radio station. It launched a new station with the call signal KCOZ-FM (more familiarly known to locals as "Cozy"). The price of the home was $23,000, just $8,000 more than its original construction cost in 1897.[80] The price tag was indicative of the poor state of the structure, but the principals endeavored to preserve the home's grand architecture. For the greater part of the next decade, the mansion provided office and studio space for the radio station. The Logan Mansion survived to be reborn in the 1990s again as another radio station, KMJJ radio. For a brief period at the turn of the twenty-first century, Shreveport Community Renewal also occupied the home.

Throughout its uses, the Logan Mansion continued to be recognized as a place of historic significance as it reflected the city's elegance and economic influence. It was, first and most important, a home, a link to the memories and history of the people who lived there and played a role in the framing of local nineteenth-century city society. Before the tragic tale of eleven-year-old Theodora Hunt intersected the Logan story, the home was simply a typical Gilded Age family residence. Afterward, it gained an eerie reputation.

The Logan Mansion has again become a family residence. Restoration work on the old home is tedious, and the daily life of the current residents is similar to, yet different from, that of Robert and Livie Logan over a century ago. The current owners had no idea that now they were also inheriting an epic ghost story with their home purchase. According to the legend and lore that has surrounded the Logan Mansion for decades, mysterious events are rather commonplace. Often, the strange occurrences have taken the form of simple acts of playful mischief. Other reports have stronger overtones, still mischievous but with more dramatic manifestations. While the stories of ghostly activity have traditionally been linked to the young Theodora Hunt or another unknown young girl, other tales seem to suggest that more than one ghostly occupant might be present.

Throughout the years, various workers, visitors and occupants of the Logan Mansion have reported paranormal activity. The current owners, the LeBrun family, have a rich and colorful history to relate to visitors regarding the home, much of it relating to their own experiences. Simple acts of childish mischief—such as misplaced items suddenly located in their original spot, doors locked from the inside while the owners were outside and strung Christmas lights suddenly and inexplicably dropping from their banister location—are all among the experiences of unexplained activity they report. Lore from the radio station era is equally rich, including the often-recounted tale that the ghostly presence of the Logan Mansion caused the station to lose its broadcast signal for an entire day when challenged to reveal itself.

Given the building's consistent history of ghostly lore, paranormal investigators were anxious to measure activity there. Brandon Thomas of Louisiana Spirits Paranormal Investigations supervised an investigation in 2007. The investigation included numerous reports of individuals experiencing extreme unease in certain places in the home, as well as reports of witnesses seeing a young girl on the premises. Paranormal investigations can be scientific in their approach. They can include the use of equipment designed to make verifiable and quantifiable measurements by activating infrared cameras, digital voice recorders and equipment to measure electromagnetic fields. From the beginning of such an investigation, experts take pains to eliminate other sources of the unexplained phenomena. They also require the owners to submit to lengthy questionnaires. Once the investigation proceeds, it becomes a professional endeavor seeking hard evidence of the paranormal.[81] In this case, the Logan Mansion investigation produced inconclusive results:

> *The investigation began in the same fashion as others: Base readings were taken, camera systems were set up, and the team prepared to go lights out. In one specific case, one of our investigators became emotional in a particular portion of the home. This was later accompanied with numerous EMF spikes and several strange noises. As we always say, personal experiences are good, yet are never enough to warrant any one place "haunted."*[82]

Even considering the inclusive nature of the paranormalists' report, the publicity surrounding the Louisiana Spirits investigation of the Logan Mansion has helped to support greater curiosity about the residence, its history and its ghostly lore. Visitors flock to the old home, perhaps to hear a ghost story or two, but in the process they learn much about the history of one of Shreveport's most interesting eras. Robert Logan lived the dream of a prosperous businessman in Shreveport in one of the finest homes on one of the finest streets in the city. Logan's is the story of many late nineteenth-century entrepreneurs in America, a story that could appear in the annals of prosperous cities across the nation during the Gilded Age.

Historical records provide insight into the lore surrounding Theodora Hunt and the validity of the often-repeated stories of her tragic demise. According to the marker on her grave in Shreveport's Greenwood Cemetery, Theodora Hunt died on June 20, 1904, just a few months short of what would have been her twelfth birthday. A simple inscription

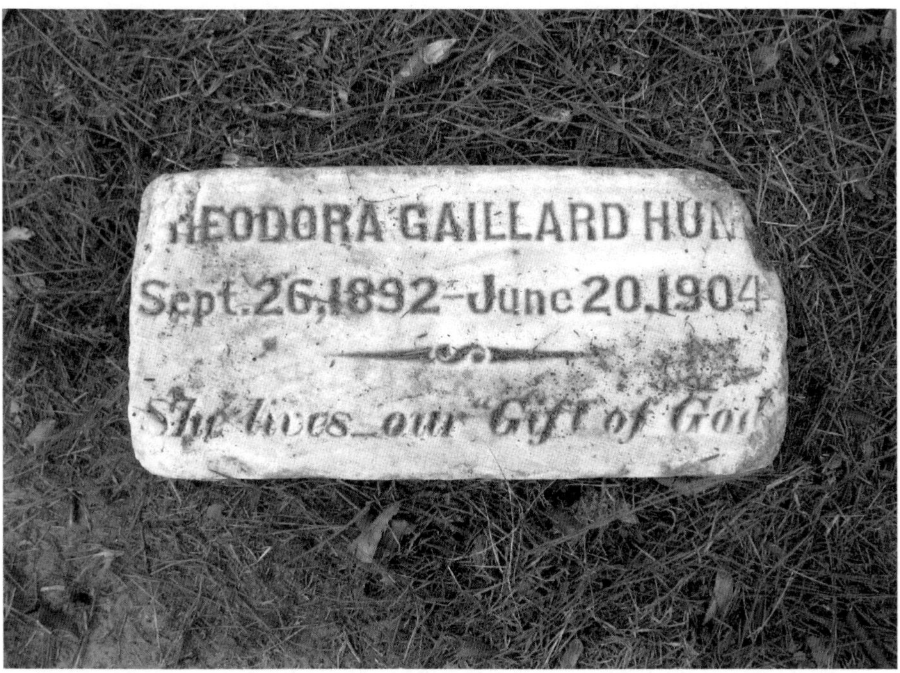

Gravestone of Theodora Hunt in Greenwood Cemetery, Shreveport, Louisiana. *Photograph by Gary D. Joiner.*

of "She Lives...Our Gift of God" represents the grief of parents who have lost a child but gives no hints about the nature of the tragedy. Others might argue that this inscription is an eerie premonition of Theodora's continued presence in the Logan Mansion, where she was reported to have leaped to death.

The *Shreveport Times* reported on June 21, 1904: "Dr. Randall Hunt was called to Hot Springs, Arkansas, by the unexpected fatal illness of his oldest daughter." The column goes on to report that Mrs. Hunt (Emily) had recently accompanied their daughter to the health resort. Theodora's death certificate notes that her cause of death was heart failure at the age of eleven years and six months.[83] Given the historical record, it is not likely that Theodora Hunt committed suicide or even that she fell or otherwise jumped from the Logan Mansion. The medical record is clear and unbiased in its report of a medical cause of death. The newspaper report suggests that no one expected Theodora's illness to be fatal, even though she was receiving medical treatment in Hot Springs, which was known for its healing waters.

Perhaps Theodora had an illness that caused her to fall—not jump—from a window in the home. The historical evidence can neither confirm nor deny this. It is impossible to refute the persistent oral tradition surrounding the circumstances of her death using historical sources. Neither can it refute this claim. History can only chronicle the verifiable story of human beings preserved in written records. Any ghosts that may or may not haunt the rooms of the Logan Mansion are far beyond the scope of the historian's scrutiny. If Theodora's ghost does roam the massive rooms and halls of the mansion, it would be quite fitting for her to stand at that third-story window and gaze across the street where her family's home once stood. Today, that view would only reveal terraced stone steps leading to a vacant lot.

What emerges from the lore and legend surrounding this magnificent old home is no less fascinating, regardless of evidence in the historical record. Residents of the city so often repeat the stories of the haunting of the Logan Mansion that they are sometimes considered fact, regardless of what truth the historian might uncover. Whether or not there are ghosts in residence, those who appreciate history can find much to recommend this grand old mansion that has survived to testify to the city's colorful past.

THE DAVIS HOMEPLACE

The Highland area of Shreveport, just north of Kings Highway, is the location of a stately old home still known as the Davis Homeplace. Named for its original family, the title is still resonant although the Davis family vacated the residence long ago. The new owners, the Gill family, have not only taken great care to retain the identity of the house and secure its history, but they have also restored it to its 1916 grandeur. Walking across the threshold into the foyer, one steps backward into time. The home displays antique furnishings and accessories that convey the ambience of an important historical era that is preserved throughout the structure. In some ways, the home is a museum of Shreveport history, encompassing the stories of many lives that touched the pages of the city's past.

The Highland neighborhood stretches for large city blocks on what was once the edge of early Shreveport expansion. In the 1920s, when the school board built C.E. Byrd High School at its present location less than a mile south of the Davis Homeplace, numerous complaints were made about the remote location of the facility. Clearly there was little development present. In fact, the area was considered rural, with fields that were home to cows and chickens.[84] Fortunately, it did not lack streetcar service, so the expansion of Shreveport continued southward. When construction began on the Davis Homeplace, the neighborhood was just beginning to reflect the unique character of the booming economy of the early twentieth century. Today, this area of Shreveport remains at the heart of the city and continues to be home to businesses and homeowners in close proximity to each other. It has consistently attracted the attention of historic preservationists with its diverse architecture.

It is not hard to imagine a ghost story or two in a neighborhood like this, and the current owners have reported enough unusual activity in the past few years to provoke the interest of paranormal investigators. These include whispered voices in the upstairs rooms, mysterious invisible hands knocking on the original glass panes of the windows overlooking the backyard and photographs of the home and its belongings revealing unusual shapes and lights. Given the home's tangible connections to the past lives of so many people, discerning the potential source of such activity poses a challenge even to ghost hunters. The history of the Davis Homeplace begins not in Shreveport but among the plantations of antebellum Mississippi.

The Davis Homeplace was part of Shreveport's growth to the south, away from the Red River. The Highland neighborhood was safe from flooding that plagued homes on and near the Red River. Built in 1916 by Ella Hunt Montgomery, the home remained in the hands of several generations of her family until 2002. Ella's daughter, Mary Walton Montgomery, married Clifton F. Davis. The Davises made this their home and gave it the name it retains today. The family's history is bound up in the rich and colorful lore of the antebellum South, and the home reflects their stories as well as those of others in Shreveport history who have been tied to it. The story of Ella Hunt Montgomery is the essence of the Old South through her journey to Shreveport with its roots in a great American saga of power, dynasty and wealth. Her story lends much to legends associated with the Davis Homeplace.

Ella Hunt Montgomery was born in 1846 in Jefferson County, Mississippi, the daughter of Abijah Hunt and his wife, Mary Agnes Walton.[85] Hunt was a cotton planter of some renown, although he owed much of his wealth to his father, David Hunt, who enjoyed a storied

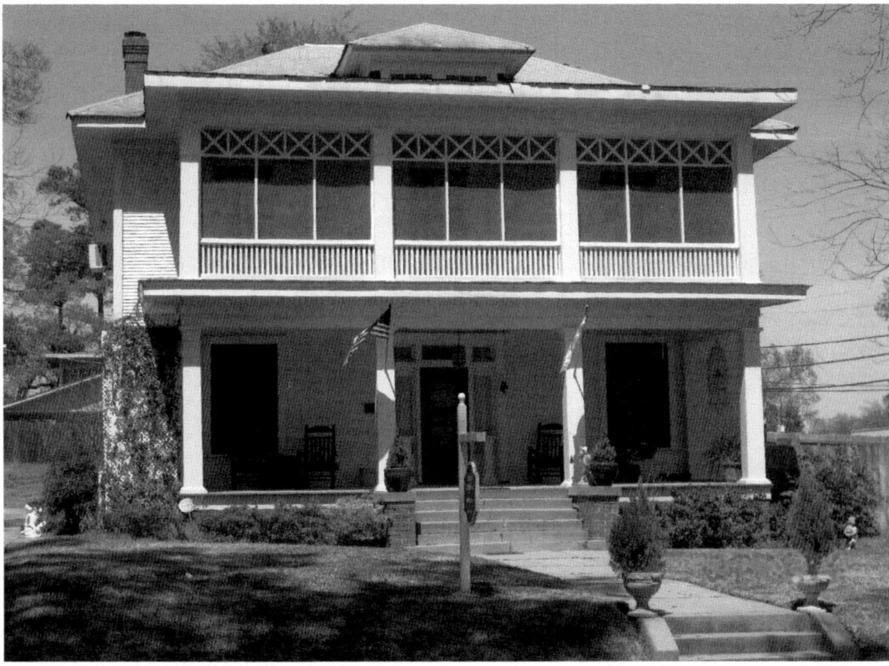

Davis Homeplace. *Photograph by Cheryl H. White.*

reputation in Mississippi. The family history traces back to Trenton, New Jersey, to the American Revolutionary War era, where David Hunt was born in 1779. The death of his father led the young Hunt to travel south to Mississippi in 1801, where he joined relatives who were successful in the merchant business. Abijah Hunt (David's uncle and namesake of his son) gave him a job as a clerk in a retail establishment in Natchez.[86]

David Hunt soon developed a reputation for hard work and frugality and, by 1803, had earned a full partnership with his uncle's firm. By then, Abijah Hunt's business encompassed five stores, making him the largest merchant in Mississippi. David was soon managing all of the merchant business and making enough money to purchase property on Cole's Creek near Natchez. He began planting cotton, but not exclusively. He preferred to raise a variety of crops, perhaps as a means of dealing with potential economic downturns. He married Mary Ann Calvit, who died from complications related to childbirth in 1810. Upon her death, the vast properties of the nearby Calviton Plantation passed to him.[87] This property included over one thousand acres of prime farmland on the Mississippi River.[88]

Soon after this tragedy, David's uncle Abijah became embroiled in a political debate involving his staunch Federalist views at a time of volatile national and state politics. A political opponent named George Poindexter shot Abijah to death in a duel in New Orleans in 1811. This unexpected turn of events led to David Hunt's inheritance of a notable portion of Abijah's business and estate. With the War of 1812 looming, David seized the opportunity to purchase the remainder of the properties from the other heirs. David Hunt invested nearly every dollar he earned into the purchase of land and earned his nickname of "King David."[89]

David's marriage to Ann Ferguson in 1816 produced some fourteen children, including Abijah Hunt, Ella Hunt Montgomery's father. The Hunt fortunes expanded almost exponentially and grew to twenty-five separate plantation properties and an estimated 1,700 slaves. Despite this wealth, Hunt remained frugal. Contemporaries reported that he selected a cherry tree from his property to use in the production of his own coffin rather than have his children purchase one from a coffin maker.[90] Although historical records do not reveal the date of Abijah's death, he predeceased his father, "King David," who died at the beginning of Civil War in May 1861. The value of his personal estate the year before he died was over $640,000.[91] David Hunt opposed secession from the federal union, but he saw it looming before it occurred. He never agreed to relinquish family holdings in Ohio because he believed they might one day provide resources for his family should the rumored secession bring about a civil conflict.[92]

The Hunt fortune must have suffered somewhat because of the war; however, Calviton Plantation was the site of Ella Hunt's wedding in February 1869. She married Field F. Montgomery and moved with him to Lake Providence, Louisiana. Field Montgomery hailed from Charlotte, Tennessee, where he was educated as a lawyer. He had moved south to Louisiana before the Civil War.[93] During the war, he served in the Fourteenth Louisiana Regiment, attaining the rank of captain before the end of the war. Records indicate he received wounds in Yorktown, Virginia, in 1862 but returned to action.[94] Following the war, he returned to East Carroll Parish, resumed his law practice and later served as district judge. The Montgomerys lived there until Field's death in 1900. By the time of the 1910 United States Census, Ella was living in Shreveport with her daughter, Mary, and her husband, Clifton Davis, a lawyer in general practice.[95]

Ella Hunt Montgomery built the home at the corner of Wilkinson Street and Line Avenue in 1916. Line Avenue was just a dirt road. Shreveport at the turn of the twentieth century and on the eve of the First World War was a bustling and active community with an economy still driven by its position on a navigable waterway. The city was growing in population and would have been a suitable place for a young lawyer like Clifton Davis to settle into a respectable practice. Clifton and Mary Montgomery Davis raised their children in the home on the corner and witnessed the transformation of this part of the city. The home reflects the development that occurred during its early history. Graceful oil lamps of the original structure had to gently defer to electricity. The garage changed from shelter for Model-T Fords to that for technologically improved automobiles. Nearly one hundred years of history passed while the house was owned by successive generations, all descendants of a remarkable dynasty that produced a Shreveport-bound female heir to the war-torn Hunt fortunes of antebellum Mississippi. This characterized the story of the Davis Homeplace until 2002, when the Gill family purchased it from a descendant.

Today, the home retains some of the belongings of generations of the Davis family and embraces the legacy of Ella Hunt Montgomery. The house also displays part of the estate of Shreveport cotton broker Captain Andrew Ingersoll and his wife, Effie Dalzell, both of whom also have significant stories. Although they never lived in the home, they are linked to the residence thanks to the Gills, who purchased items from their estate. Their portraits grace the walls of the Davis Homeplace's front room, and their treasured belongings (including the gold pocket watch of Captain Ingersoll) can be seen there. The portraits of Effie Dalzell's parents, the Reverend William Dickinson Dalzell and his wife, Estelle Logan, hang on the walls. Reverend Dalzell was the first rector of the historic St. Mark's Episcopal Church (now Church of the Holy Cross)

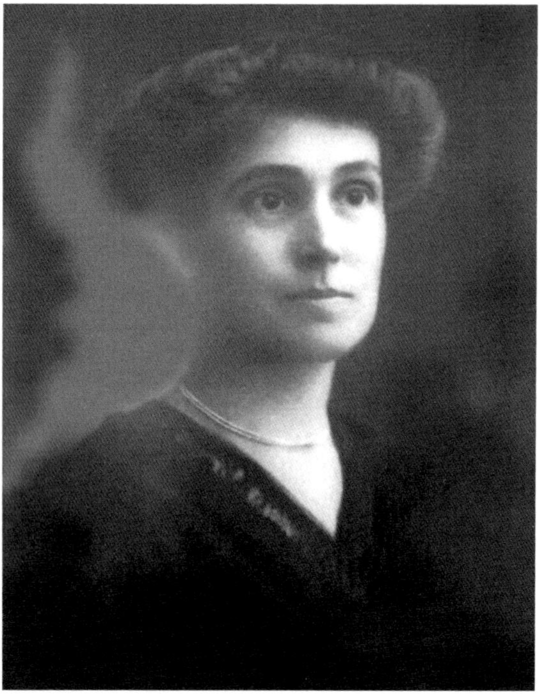

Photograph of Effie Dalzell Ingersoll in the Davis Homeplace Collection. *Photograph by Cheryl H. White.*

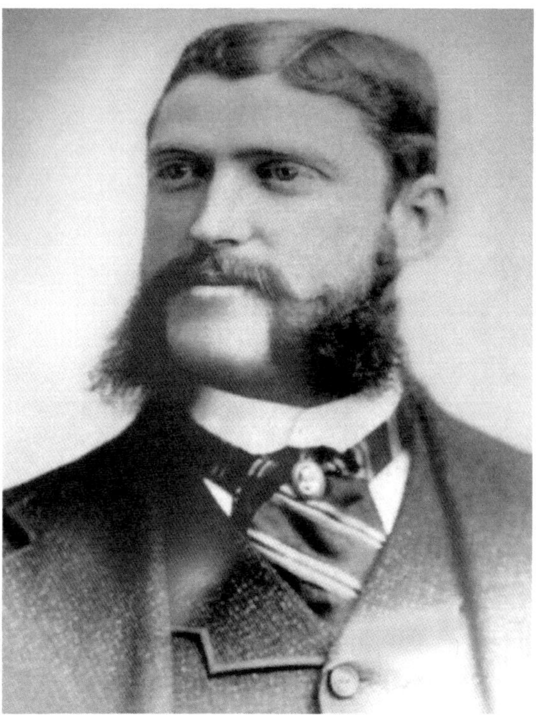

Photograph of Captain Andrew Jackson Ingersoll in the Davis Homeplace Collection. *Photograph by Cheryl H. White.*

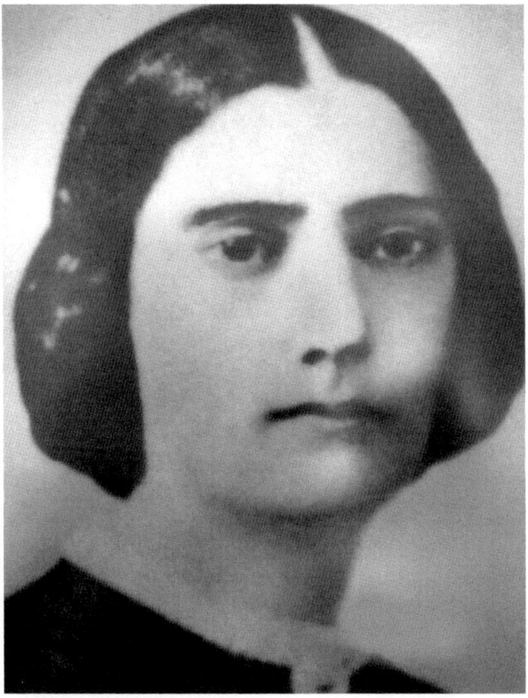

Photograph of Estelle Logan Dalzell in the Davis Homeplace Collection. *Photograph by Cheryl H. White.*

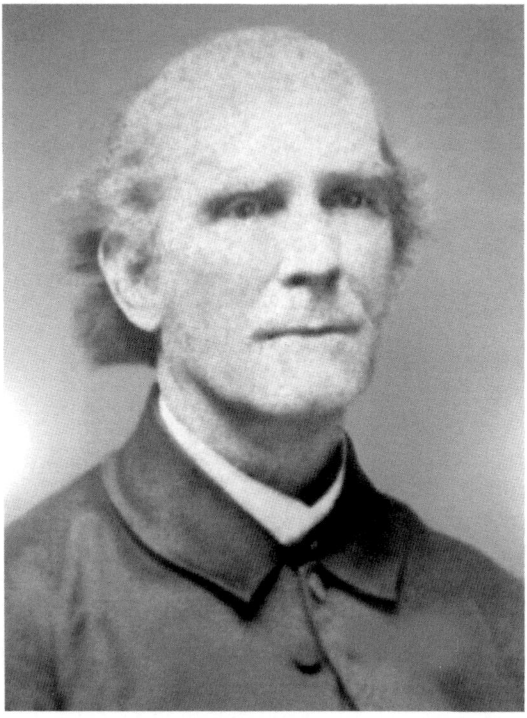

Photograph of Reverend William Dalzell in the Davis Homeplace Collection. *Photograph by Cheryl H. White.*

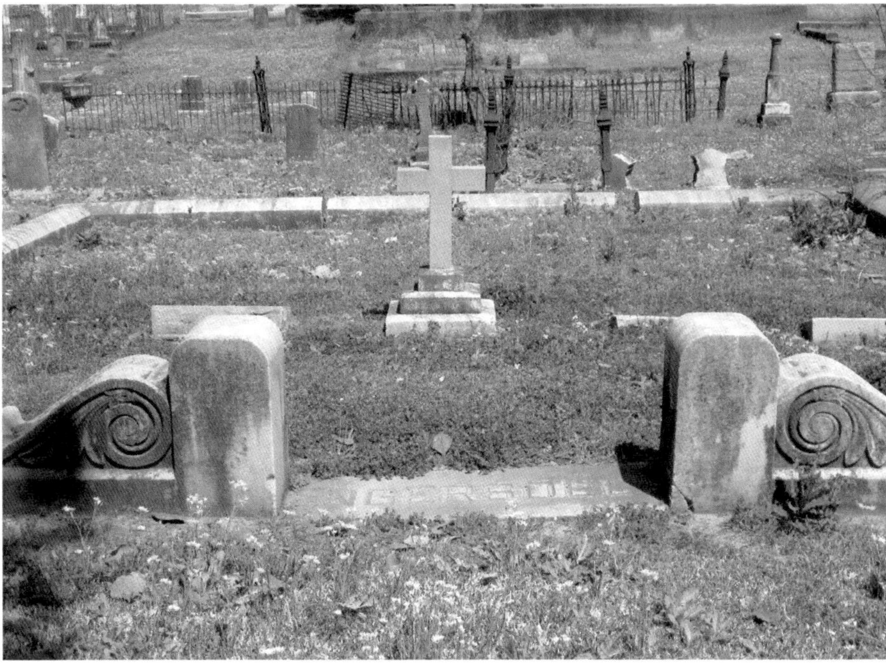

The Ingersoll family plot in Oakland Cemetery. *Photograph by Cheryl H. White.*

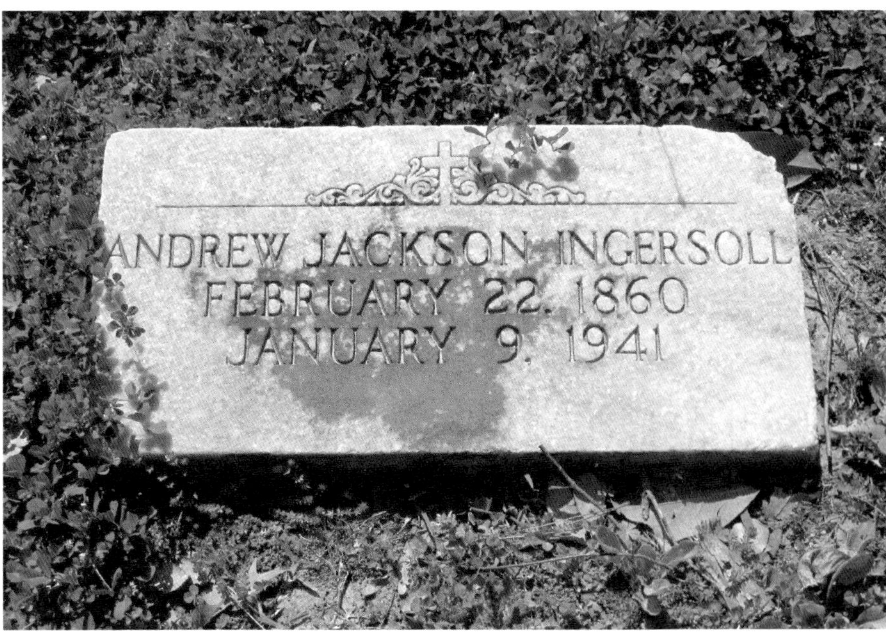

The gravestone of Captain Andrew Jackson Ingersoll. *Photograph by Cheryl H. White.*

located in downtown Shreveport. The stories of these people, despite lacking original connections to the structure, add much to the life and lore of the old Davis Homeplace.

William Dickinson Dalzell was a Jamaica-born and Oxford-educated Anglican priest and physician, born in 1828. His service as a chaplain to a Texas regiment during the Civil War eventually brought him to Shreveport in 1866.[96] From 1862 to 1865, Dalzell served as rector of St. Mark's Episcopal Church in San Antonio, where he had transferred from Christ Episcopal Church in Houston.[97] In 1866, Dalzell married Estelle Logan of New Orleans. His service as rector at St. Mark's Episcopal Church in Shreveport placed him in the very center of the yellow fever epidemic that swept through the city with ferocity in 1873.[98] Reverend Dalzell refused to leave the city during the epidemic. Instead, he opened the church to the ill and worked among them. As a physician and a

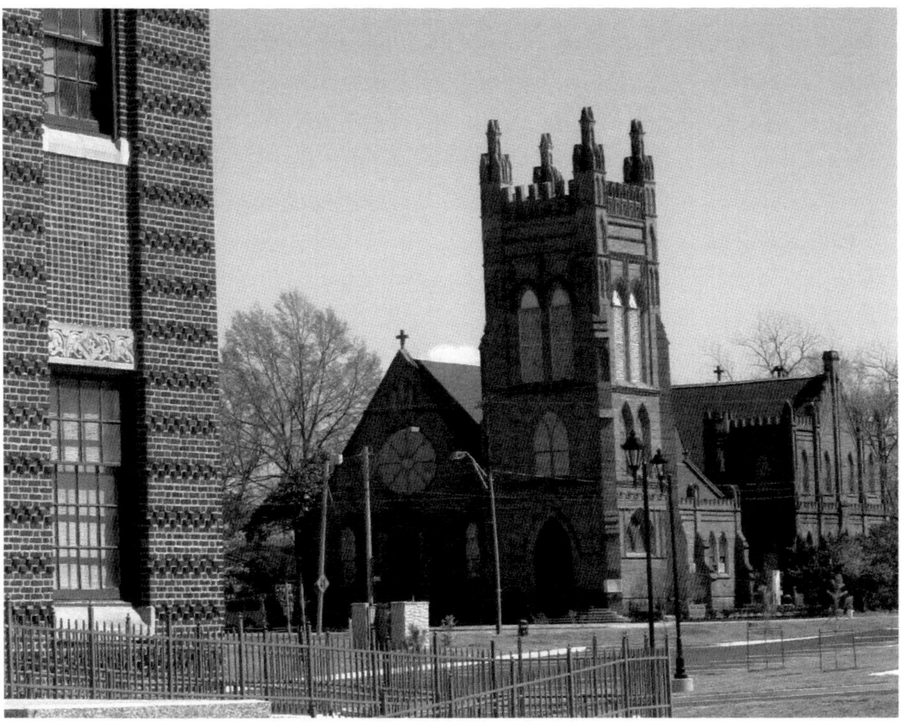

Church of the Holy Cross, formerly St. Mark's Episcopal Church, seen from Municipal Auditorium. *Photograph by Gary D. Joiner.*

clergyman, his unique dual training was valuable among the sick and the dying in Shreveport during that tragic summer. The city honored his efforts to alleviate Shreveport's suffering. Dalzell Street in Shreveport bears his name.

Reverend Dalzell's daughter, Effie Dalzell, married Captain Andrew Jackson (A.J.) Ingersoll in 1896. He was a prominent cotton broker in Shreveport, affectionately called "Captain Jack."[99] His story was representative of many who came to Shreveport during this period, drawn by the allure of a booming commercial city where fortunes could be made. Andrew Jackson Ingersoll was born in 1860 in Mobile, Alabama, to middle-class merchant parents. In 1880, he was still living in Mobile working as a telegraph operator.[100] He must have come to Shreveport shortly thereafter and inherited his father's gift for the merchant trade. According to census data, the value of the Ingersoll home in Shreveport in 1930 was $35,000, a healthy sum during the Great Depression.

The personalities of these individuals are imprinted on to the Davis Homeplace. Their portraits grace the walls, and it has been said that their spirits visit as well. Haunted locations are sites that seem to reflect the great human drama. Paranormal theorists suggest that objects can become powerful triggers for energy attachment, and in this way, collections of personal belongings may encourage a haunting in a particular place.[101]

Because the Davis Homeplace's history mirrors the development of the city, it provides for paranormal speculation and investigation. Increasingly, this Shreveport landmark draws the curious and ghost hunters. Mary Montgomery Davis's wedding dress is displayed on an upstairs landing, beautifully preserved since its use for her wedding to Clifton Davis in 1897. Captain Ingersoll's gold pocket watch has a place of prominence in a dining room curio cabinet. These articles are of interest in and of themselves, apart from any reports of ghosts.

Soon after the Gills purchased the Davis Homeplace in 2002, strange and unexplained events began to occur. During a Highland Restoration Association tour, many touring the home heard the unexplained sound of a woman's laughter in a room where no one was present. Both owners have reported hearing voices whispering in empty rooms adjacent to these. An unseen hand frantically rapping on a window overlooking the backyard seemingly was said to have saved the Gills' daughter from an encounter with three snakes living in the overgrown conditions soon after they moved in. The owners believe that if the home is haunted by ghosts of previous inhabitants or visitors, these are kind spirits that are either reluctant to leave the gracious home or are trying to tell them something.

The owners invited paranormal investigators who have recorded five separate electronic voice phenomena (EVP) recordings. They identified something including what seems to be a man's voice uttering, "No way." Most of the activity recorded was in the home's first-floor music room. The owners have no fear of living in what some might term a "haunted" house. They seem to enjoy the past that resonates through their home. Any ghosts that reside at the Davis Homeplace must be comfortable with the furnishings and atmosphere, from the familiar working transoms to original oil lamps. Perhaps by preserving the past in such a way, the Gills allow Davis Homeplace to attract and retain its ghosts as permanent guests.

In many ways, the Davis Homeplace is a metaphor for Shreveport's unique historical intersection of diverse personalities, each with a claim to distinct contributions to the overall character of the city. As home to historic artifacts, personal memorabilia, antiques and portraits that preserve the images of the past, it represents a means of keeping the past alive. To touch the gold pocket watch once held by "Captain Jack" is to remember the days when cotton was king and steamboats graced the Red River. The intricate lace of a century-old wedding dress makes real the timeless hopes and dreams of a young woman not unlike any living today; it evokes a common experience that transcends the decades. With so much life and living represented within the walls of this magnificent old home, how could even the dead remain silent?

THE FORBING GHOST

Approaching the Shreveport city limits in the southeast, the traveler encounters the almost forgotten community of Forbing, an area known more for its legendary railroad ghost than for its nineteenth-century namesake, Hiram Forbing. Natives of the north Louisiana area are well acquainted with the popular lore surrounding the mysterious railroad crossing at Forbing and its ghost or, depending on the version of the story, more than one ghost. Knowledgeable natives can offer more than one version of the tale, since it has evolved through decades of telling and experience. As is the case with many similar haunting tales across the country, many residents claim to have experienced the supernatural at this locally famous railroad crossing. However, among those who say they have seen the elusive Forbing Ghost, none of the tales is consistent regarding the origin of the haunting there.

For decades, what was once considered a remote railroad crossing has attracted those with an earnest desire to experience the paranormal. The crossing has been the site of an almost ritualized rite of passage for area youth who often travel to the tracks at midnight in search of spine-tingling adventure. A fascinating aspect of this particular tale relates to the phenomenon of suggestibility. Many claim to have experienced a ghostly

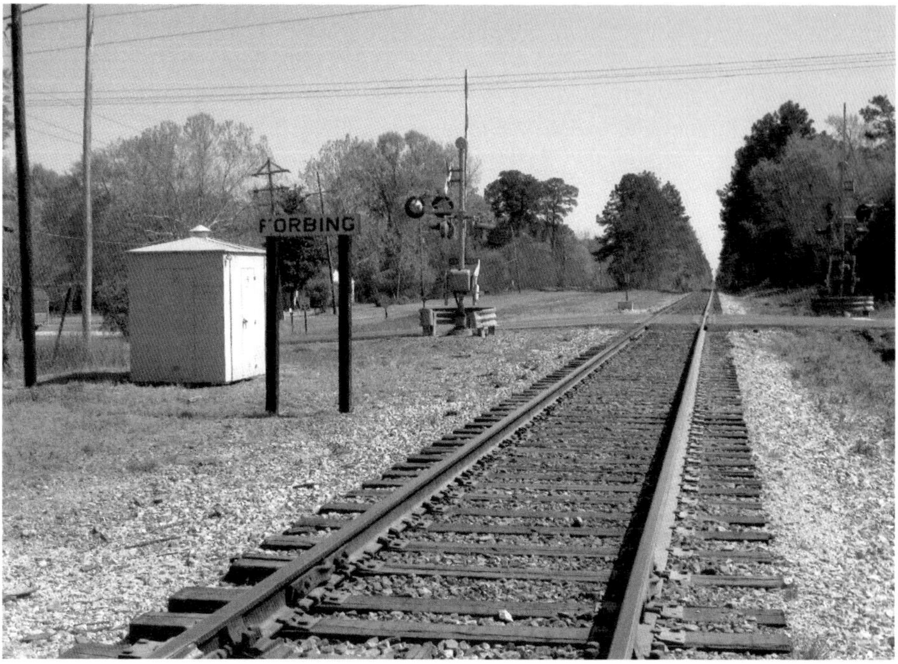

The railroad crossing at Forbing, Louisiana. *Photograph by Cheryl H. White.*

encounter at this location despite the lack of any historical evidence that a tragedy occurred there. The lack of historical substantiation has not deterred the proliferation of this popular tale.

Suggestibility is a feature associated with the Forbing Ghost perhaps more than any other local legend or tale. This term refers to the tendency of an individual to be persuaded that a given experience is real in spite of a lack of evidence. Local tales abound that feature the personal experiences of those people who have seen or experienced this ghost. It seems that anyone visiting the tracks with a predisposition to believe will likely have an encounter with the supernatural. The psychological basis for this is simple: people interpret their surroundings and the sensory input they receive based on what is familiar.[102] This tale is so familiar that it happens to have taken on the mantle of truth.

The only historical connection of the Forbing Ghost tale to the city of Shreveport is its link to the community's early development and its placement along the railroad lines that traverse northern Louisiana, going into and out of Shreveport. Although much of what was originally Forbing, Louisiana, is now within the city limits of Shreveport, the name once designated only a sleepy agricultural settlement just south of town. Historically speaking, the area bears little significance, but its origins incorporate common themes of the post–Civil War era of the American South and the predominantly agricultural economy of the area in the late nineteenth century. Like many places that developed in the same era, the fertile farmlands beckoned both farmers and commercial interests that based their businesses on marketing the fruits of the soil. Shreveport was already a major port of passage on the Red River by the time Forbing emerged as an agricultural settlement.

Hiram Forbing was born in 1845 in Indiana and fought for the Union. He enlisted in May 1861 as part of Company F in the Indiana Twelfth Infantry Regiment and mustered out in May 1862 in Washington, D.C.,[103] moving to north Louisiana some time after the Civil War. Forbing was living in north Louisiana by 1871, since he appears as the defendant in a legal battle of that year involving 219 acres of land he purchased in a disputed family succession. The case reached the Louisiana Supreme Court before he received a decision in his favor.[104] He and his wife, Louisa, appear on the 1880 United States Census, living in the eighth ward of Caddo Parish, Louisiana.[105] He was apparently a successful farmer and by 1910 had a household with four children.[106] When Hiram Forbing died on Christmas Day 1932, he was eighty-nine years old and had risen to such a position of influence as a wealthy planter that the area of southern Caddo Parish today bears his name.[107]

During the decades he lived in Louisiana, Hiram Forbing would have witnessed much in terms of progress, including the construction of the railroads. It is from the story of the rails that some of the most consistent lore surrounding haunted Shreveport emerges, in the form of a legend known as the Forbing Ghost. This story, which has a unique resonance with those in other towns scattered throughout the United States, shares a common theme related to the great historical mystique of the rails. Because similar stories are found in towns all over America, perhaps they demonstrate a need to cling to a nostalgic era, even though many have no historic foundation. This underscores the allure of the past and a

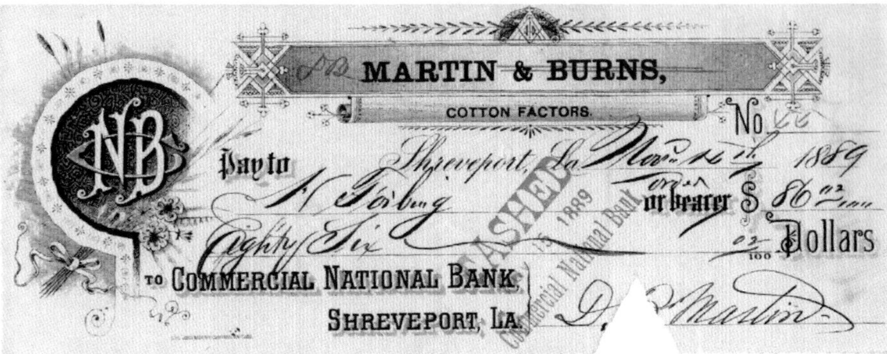

Obverse scan of Commercial National Bank draft from Martin & Burns cotton factors, to Hiram Forbing, dated November 14, 1889. *Collection of Ernie Roberson.*

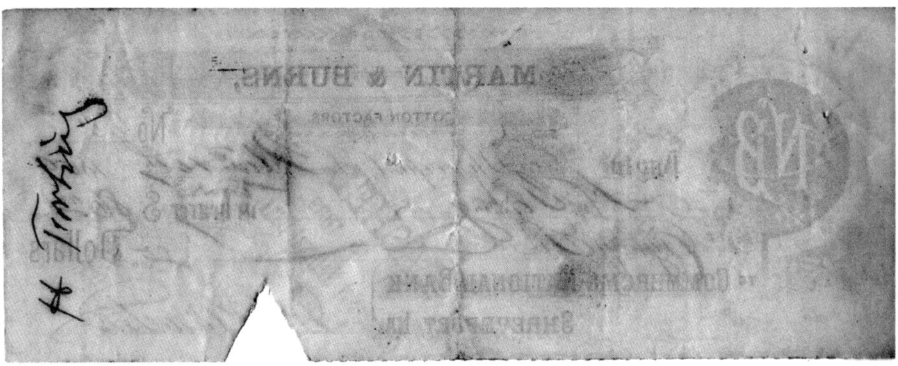

Reverse scan of Commercial National Bank draft from Martin & Burns cotton factors, to Hiram Forbing, dated November 14, 1889. *Collection of Ernie Roberson.*

common need for cultural identification as people attempt to preserve history through shared folklore.

The first railroad through Shreveport entered from the west when the Vicksburg, Shreveport and Texas Railroad Company was designed to connect Shreveport with neighboring Marshall in east Texas. Engineers surveyed the route in 1853, and construction may have begun as early as 1855, but the United States Civil War caused construction plans to cease temporarily. Although workers had graded much of the track near Shreveport, work on the rails was far from complete. General Edmund Kirby Smith worked to locate additional rail to complete the tracks during the war, because Shreveport was a significant target of the Union as the gateway to Texas. By 1873, the Texas and Pacific Railroad had completed a connection between Shreveport and Dallas.[108] From that point forward, the railroad shaped the history of the city.

The railroad tracks that run through Forbing and cross Flournoy-Lucas Road have produced a legend that is difficult to trace, even though it has existed for decades. The legend has several different variations. The first version tells the tale of a brakeman whose job was to hold up a burning lantern as a warning to any approaching train at night. At some point, the brakeman realized that the lantern had blown out, so he frantically worked to relight it as he heard the whistle of an oncoming train in the distance. The lighted warning to the other train did not come in time, and this version of the legend reports a collision with the other train that killed the brakeman instantly. According to this story, he walks on the tracks at Forbing in darkness, swinging his lantern. Even today, some residents claim that brave observers can view the lantern light precisely at midnight.

A second version of the Forbing Ghost legend involves a school bus filled with children that supposedly stalled on the tracks at Forbing one morning. According to the legend, several children on board the bus died instantly when an approaching train slammed into the vehicle. Those who tell the story maintain that people in cars parked on the tracks even today report that those long-dead schoolchildren mysteriously "push" the cars off the tracks and out of harm's way. Another aspect of the legend alleges that one can see the physical evidence of these ghosts by dusting the trunk of the car with talcum powder or other dust as, apparently, these ghosts even leave behind their fingerprints!

A third version of the Forbing Ghost involves a tale about an unnamed man who was decapitated by an oncoming train at the tracks, while another variation claims the train impact actually severed his hand and that he bled to death on the tracks. As the legend goes, his lantern is visible from the crossing as he walks the tracks at midnight, apparently searching for his lost head. Yet another story surrounding the Forbing railroad crossing is that of a young lawyer who committed suicide by walking in front of an oncoming train.[109]

Historical inquiry into the possibility of links for these very different legends is actually quite disappointing. No version of the story appears to have any basis in the historical record. There are no reports of a train wreck at Forbing, nor is there any evidence of a collision involving a train and a school bus. What makes this legend particularly fascinating is that, unlike other haunted stories from Shreveport, this one is not related to real events or people that would lend credibility to the tale. The complete lack of historical verification for the legend of this ghost places it as pure fiction.

The true mystery of the Forbing Ghost is not verification of a haunting there but why the stories began. It may be that residents who like a good story heard one or two from other locales. Railroad legend and lore across the United States yield similar stories. Just south of San Antonio, Texas, in a neighborhood near the historic San Juan mission, one tale recounts that an intersection of rail and highway was the site of a train collision involving a school bus full of children. This story, like of the one involving the Forbing Ghost tracks, is decades old, dating to at least the 1940s. Like the local tale, it includes a version with the pushing of cars from the tracks to safety by ghostly schoolchildren.[110]

The story of a train accident with a similar description as this one appeared in a December 1938 article in *TIME* magazine. The place was neither Forbing, Louisiana, nor San Antonio, Texas. It involved the small town of Midvale, Utah. On December 1, 1938, a school bus full of children collided with a freight train of the Denver and Rio Grande Western Railroad. The impact killed twenty-two of the thirty-eight children aboard. Snow and fog reportedly obscured the driver's visibility. The same *TIME* magazine article from December 1938 relates a similar incident that happened just the day before in Wisconsin, again involving a school bus.[111] The stories from Utah and Wisconsin are true. What is fascinating is how that version of events became part of the railroad lore of several towns that never even experienced such a tragedy. Researchers have found no evidence of any similar train tragedy in either Forbing or San Antonio. Even a much publicized debunking of this train track ghost story in the media did little to dissuade onlookers and ghost hunters from traveling to these locations to experience the stories firsthand.[112]

Haunted railroad stories prove popular in Clark County, Arkansas, near the town of Gurdon. There, the legend reports a light that floats above the railroad tracks, supposedly the ghost of a railroad worker who was decapitated in a freak accident and now searches eternally for his head. A similar tale is popular from Saratoga, Texas, at the Bragg Road Light. On a walkway that once functioned as a track bed for the Santa Fe Railroad, a flickering yellow light is reported to be seen at night, mysteriously changing to red. Local legend contends that this light comes from the lantern of a ghost brakeman, also decapitated and searching for his head. From Michigan's Upper Peninsula comes the tale of the Paulding Light, which locals report to be the ghost of either a brakeman or an engineer.[113]

Nowhere in the country has the story of the phantom lantern been more famous than in Maco, North Carolina, a town that claims a strange light directly over the railroad crossing at Maco Station. It also shares many of the same characteristics and details as other haunted railroad stories; however, what is interesting is that it appears to be much older than versions related elsewhere in the United States. It may serve as the point of origin for the lantern legends. Folklore regarding the haunted crossing at Maco dates to the end of the Civil War, perhaps as early as 1873. It involves a rail worker named Joe Baldwin who died by decapitation in a crash between two trains.[114]

In addition to urban legends like these that involve American railways are stories about ghost trains that travel throughout the countryside. One legend from Colorado tells of a phantom steam locomotive reportedly seen regularly at Marshall Pass. There is a also a legend from railroad history about the ghost train of President Lincoln that travels through New York State each April carrying his coffin and a funeral orchestra. These similar tales raise important sociological questions regarding the purpose of such lore in our historical consciousness.

What is it about railroads that produce such vivid accounts, firing the imagination with tales of ghostly engineers, phantom trains and deadly crossings? How is that similar tales travel from place to place throughout the United States, most with no basis in historical record? Why did the legend of a ghost evolve at the tracks at Forbing and not in another area of the city? Is it only that someone decades ago once heard the tale from a distant locale and repeated it, superimposing the name of Forbing on the legend and giving it new life in a new place? There is no question that the repeating of the tale throughout the decades has helped cement its place firmly in Shreveport's folklore. However, it is important to recognize that merely repeating an oft-told tale does not make it accurate, and it certainly does not negate the need for historical confirmation.

The story of the Forbing Ghost is not founded on evidence, but it retains a place in the rich fabric of this city's past because it provides a firm connection to the great era of the railroads. The railroad was the first efficient means of moving people and goods across the vast lands of the ever-expanding United States at the turn of the twentieth century. The history of America's railroads is a uniquely colorful one, full of adventure, enterprise, challenges and intrigue. The railroad and the dramatic changes that it brought to the nation touched upon virtually every aspect of society. It also became big business in America, producing some of the most famous capitalist barons in history and eventually requiring government intervention to correct economic abuses. It is no wonder that this aspect of our history has produced such colorful folklore, as it touched virtually every aspect of society.

Complex systems of interstate highways and advances in freight shipping and air travel have combined to supplant the supremacy of the railways in the American story. Perhaps the passing of this remarkable era of history produced myriad legends as a means of holding on to the past and ensuring that people of future ages would not forget. In this way, folklore connects people to the real history and forges a genuine bond even amid the mythical and mysterious.

Railroad history transected nineteenth-century Shreveport just as it did in communities all across America. The rails are the true iron and steel manifestations of a nation's determination and hard work; yet again, the lore that produced these often similar tales results from the energy of the lives that shaped a dynamic period in American history. What the historical investigator can state with accuracy is that the Forbing railroad crossing today stands as a testament that the folklore of a place links with its history, but not always in an objectively measurable way.

As for the Forbing Ghost, it is indeed a real phenomenon, measured best not by the paranormal experts but rather by the social scientists who find compelling evidence of a shared national identity in other railroad "ghosts." It represents a contagion of popular lore that has somehow spread from one community to the next, adapted locally and been retold and reinvented. One can say that the Forbing Ghost exists all across America, in a local incarnation of a familiar theme and one that resonates with the allure of the past.

Therefore, it is true that on any given night, someone will visit this old railroad crossing with the expectation of an encounter with the Forbing Ghost. If one looks in earnest for the mysterious swinging lantern down the track or waits for the gentle hands of ghost children to push their car off the tracks, then this remote stretch of railroad will not disappoint, if only in the imagination. And that is as good a reason for an interesting story as any other.

THE CADDO PARISH PENAL FARM

Just to the west of Shreveport, near the Shreveport Regional Airport, is a popular haunted spot that attracts the curious and adventurous. What remains of the old parish correctional facility, the Caddo Parish Penal Farm, stands abandoned and deteriorating. Constructed in 1905 to house minimum-security offenders in a self-supporting agricultural environment, the penal farm is a brick-and-mortar witness to a harsher time in corrections history. This haunted site tells three quite different tales—one of prison conditions in the South during the first half of the twentieth century; another of an unlikely African American lieutenant governor who profoundly impacted Louisiana history; and another of a famous female artist whose work found inspiration among the convicts who once worked the land at the farm. All of these vivid histories never transected, yet each touches upon the others in a remarkable way. The haunted penal farm bears silent witness to them all.

Throughout most of the year, the old site of weathered brick buildings is secluded by trees and reachable only on foot through broken fences, deep brush and thickets of vines. Yet the seclusion of the facility has not discouraged curious ghost hunters who are convinced that the site is haunted by convicts of the past, their voices moaning through the woods at night. Indeed, the current state and appearance of the facility seem a natural setting for ghost stories. The buildings have fallen into serious disrepair and increasingly reflect decades of disuse and lack of maintenance. The buildings are vine-covered and covered with extensive graffiti, stark testimony to the abandonment of the site. Many in the area believe a legend that prisoners at the penal farm suffered mistreatment and torture at the hands of their guards, but there is little evidence to support this claim. Another local legend claims that the basement of the facility housed an electric chair. This is not true, but the presentation of historical facts is not likely to discourage those who are determined to promote this popular local legend.

From the time it was abandoned as an incarceration facility for the parish, Caddo Parish retained ownership of the penal farm, and despite attempts to post the property and isolate it from curiosity seekers, curiosity seekers are not deterred. The allure of old abandoned places both beckons and inspires fear. Empty structures seem to echo the past, as natural curiosity emerges when people step into these places and ask questions. In this case, questions might be these: Who lived here? What crimes did they commit? How did their lives end? Anyone who seeks clues in the old penal farm will hear answers only in the wind through the open windows and doors, and perhaps the occasional scurry of an insect or rodent. It is a place where imagination can have free reign.

Any local teenager who has visited this popular "dare" spot can offer a fascinating array of paranormal experiences, including the most common manifestation of unexplained moans and cries and voices speaking in the now empty rooms. An occasional visitor has also reported sightings of men clothed in stereotypical striped convict uniforms, but it is not clear that Caddo Parish ever issued this type of clothing to prisoners. Given the facility's remote location and its overgrown and deteriorating condition, it is not difficult to imagine it as the setting for ghost stories. The history of the facility, as well as that of interesting historical figures associated with it, provide additional fodder for the promotion of legend.

The stories of hauntings at the Caddo Parish Penal Farm may attract the amateur ghost hunter, but its history attracts historians. Fascinating stories of Louisiana history are connected with the legends of the haunted Pea Farm, including that of Reconstruction lieutenant governor Caesar Carpentier "C.C" Antoine and Clyde Connell, a noted twentieth-century artist. Richly interwoven into the local folklore of this haunted place are their stories. The very existence of the abandoned old prison invites historians to inquire into the often-brutal history of incarceration in Louisiana at a time when the state was already infamous for the bloodiest prison in the United States (Angola State Penitentiary). The early twentieth century in Louisiana was enlightened in rehabilitative correction theory among prison populations, particularly in the South. Perhaps the state's reputation in this regard has done much to increase the superstition surrounding such places. The stories of mistreatment at the facility, although unverifiable, could likely to be true.

The prison farm system originated in the post-Reconstruction era in the South, where state and local governments often put convicts to use for economic purposes. In settings such as this, convicts worked to produce the food for their own consumption and also sold produce to specified markets or to the public at large. The Thirteenth Amendment to the U.S. Constitution ended the practice of slavery and involuntary servitude, except as punishment for a crime. This unique period of United States history witnessed the interesting transition from a system of chattel slavery to a legal system that allowed the same type of servitude in the penal system.

Although the Civil War had no direct impact on the penal philosophies of the American South, the outcome of that conflict meant that, for the first time, significant numbers of blacks entered the public correctional systems. Former slaves became free citizens and, as such, became subject to institutionalized punishments if they engaged in criminal behavior. These realities of the post–Civil War South created the environment for a two-pronged approach to incarceration in the convict-lease system and the penal farm system. Although the leasing of convicts was not a long-lasting practice of governments in the South, the development of the penal farm agricultural model became a core approach for the correctional concept, one that today continues in Louisiana's prison ethic.[115]

While the Progressive era of the early twentieth century witnessed some initiatives for prison reform, these efforts seem slow by today's standards. A major target of social progressives at the close of the nineteenth century was the abolition of the popular convict-lease system used in many southern states. This system, although closely related to the concept of a penal farm, was much harsher in its application. States effectively leased laborers to private enterprises, providing the dual benefit of revenues to the state and inexpensive labor to the farm or business. Between 1890 and 1917, seven southern states abolished the convict-lease system in response to strong social pressure.[116] However, efforts continued to justify the use of the penal farm model, as evidenced by the existence of these institutions well into the twentieth century. A popular sociological work in 1939 surveying the state of the American prison contrasted southern prisons with those of the north. It reported, "The prison systems and conditions in the South are different because of the climate and the existence of the race problem."[117]

The Caddo Parish Penal Farm earned the nickname the "Pea Farm" partly because "pea" is an abbreviated form of the word "penal" and also, due to its primarily agricultural nature, convicts sustained themselves through growing their own vegetables, including peas. It is not clear that peas were ever the staple produce of the farm, but nevertheless, the name became permanently etched into the site's identity in the local vernacular.

The facility is located on lands that had once been the property of Caesar Carpentier Antoine, a Reconstruction-era African American lieutenant governor of Louisiana. The area that composed his farmlands just west of Shreveport now is home to a large auto production facility and an electric plant as well. Only the old penal farm remains obscured in overgrowth and abundant forest, much of it with new pine forest not more than a few decades old. A stroll through the landscape reveals old streambeds, massive oak trees of significant age and the gentle slope of what were likely fertile fields juxtaposed with the cluttered trash of frequent visitors. Neither the abandoned brick structures nor the land itself yields any secrets to someone who explores the property during the day, but both can provoke many questions about the past.

The story of how an African American came to possess so much rich farmland at the end of the Civil War in Louisiana is quite fascinating. C.C. Antoine's ascent to political office is a story that is rare in the late

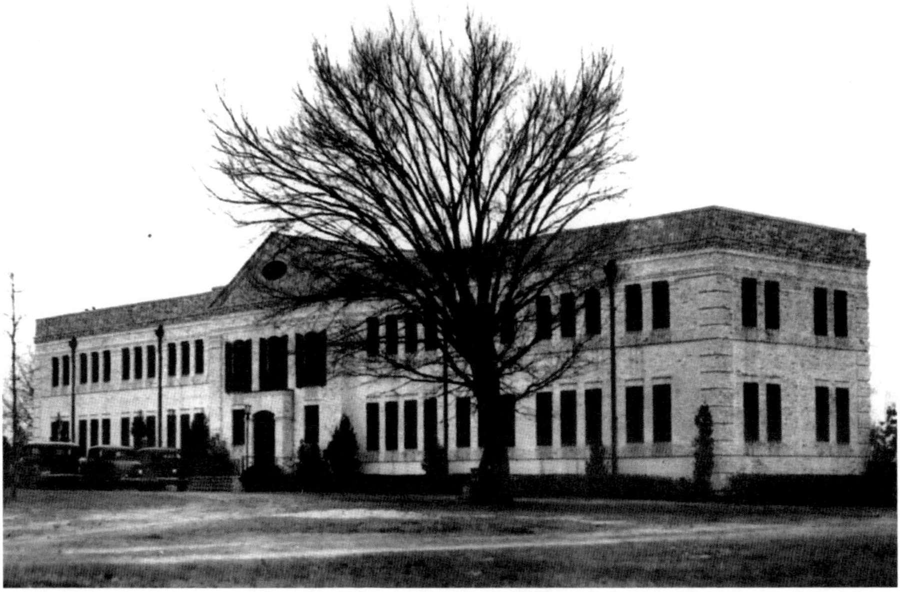

The Caddo Parish Penal Farm main building, January 26, 1935. *Courtesy of Archives and Special Collections, Louisiana State University in Shreveport. Eric J. Brock collection.*

nineteenth century. Born in 1836 in New Orleans to parents who were both Creole and free persons of color, he spent his childhood there and received a private education. Upon completion of formal education, he became a barber, since this was one of the few trades open to people of color, even in an international city like New Orleans.[118] When the Civil War erupted and Union troops occupied New Orleans, Antoine enlisted in the now famous all-black Seventh Louisiana Infantry (Louisiana Native Guards) in 1863, attaining the rank of captain before his discharge.[119] At the end of the war, he moved his family to Shreveport. His story seems to indicate a moderate amount of family wealth, certainly enough to ensure a private education as an adolescent. Prewar census records do not provide this evidence of his family's wealth. However, by 1870, his real estate in Shreveport was valued at $2,000.[120]

Antoine's significant business success likely spurred his decision to enter politics in a major way, although there is evidence that this idea had already been with him for several years. While still in New Orleans, Antoine forged strong political connections among the rising Republican

Party leadership. These ties bore fruit in 1867 when he served as a delegate to the Louisiana Constitutional Convention. Elected state senator from Caddo Parish in 1868, Antoine served in that office until 1872. Meanwhile, he continued business dealings in New Orleans as well. He had business links to other noted African American politicians, including P.B.S. Pinchback, with whom he shared a variety of business enterprises. Records indicate that he made a significant profit on the sale of lands to the city of New Orleans during this time.[121]

In 1872, C.C. Antoine was the Republican nominee for lieutenant governor of Louisiana. His previous business and political partner, Pinchback, formed an alternative ticket for the Republican Party but eventually supported Antoine out of fear that a three-way contest might ensure a Democratic victory. Numerous scandals and allegations of voter fraud rocked the election, and President Ulysses Grant's intervention helped to secure Antoine's victory. Nevertheless, Antoine's tenure as lieutenant governor was an uneasy one, fraught with conflict and criticism from the old Creole class of New Orleans.[122]

The 1876 election produced even greater scandal. Antoine's reelection bid ended with the withdrawal of federal troops from Louisiana following the hotly contested and controversial presidential election involving Rutherford Hayes that year. Across the South, the Reconstruction Republican governments toppled one by one, and Antoine's political career all but ended as a result. When he returned to Caddo Parish, he served as a member of the local school board, the final installment of his political life. His political legacy continues to be the subject of a great deal of historical criticism and controversy, and his personal ethics and integrity continue to be scrutinized. His last political effort involved the dispute over a new Jim Crow law in 1890 in Louisiana that required "separate but equal" seating on railroads for blacks and whites. Antoine was one of the predominantly Creole New Orleans committee members who organized to dispute the legislation, ultimately resulting in the often-cited *Plessey v. Ferguson* ruling by the United States Supreme Court.[123]

Although C.C. Antoine disappeared from the Louisiana political landscape by the end of the nineteenth century, his business dealings in Caddo Parish continued to distinguish him. Clear evidence of his personal wealth is demonstrated by his purchase of large amounts of land in western Caddo Parish throughout the 1880s, including where the decaying brick and mortar remains of the Caddo Parish Penal Farm lie. When he died in 1921, his accomplishments were almost forgotten in Louisiana history. The graveyard of Missionary Baptist Church is the site of what was once his unmarked grave. Antoine's final resting place lies within sight of his once expansive plantation lands, including the penal farm. His obituary received front-page placement in the local newspaper, which noted, "Interment will be at Flournoy, Louisiana, where Antoine formerly owned a large amount of land, including the present site of the parish farm."[124] On Memorial Day 1999, local historians and officials supervised the placement of a permanent tombstone marking his grave. The marker notes his contribution of service to the Union army and his service to the people of Louisiana.[125]

Yet another remarkable Louisiana resident is tied to the Caddo Parish Penal Farm: renowned artist Clyde Connell. Millie Clyde Dixon was born in 1901 in the small town of Belcher, Louisiana. The future artist lived in a large multigenerational family in a rural farmhouse, a situation that was typical of the age. The Dixon homeplace grew during the first decades of the twentieth century, a sprawling Belcher plantation where she lived for the first half of her life. Growing up in the rural South during the early twentieth century exposed Clyde to the realities of racial disparity. Later in her life, she recalled the memories of lynchings that took place near her home. These memories later found expression in her unique artwork.[126]

In 1922, Clyde married Thomas Dixon Connell, the son of another Belcher-area farmer. The newlyweds lived on the Dixon plantation and began raising a family there, one that expanded to include three children. Clyde eventually found plantation life dull, so she enrolled in weekly art classes at St. Vincent's Academy in Shreveport. As both her talent and passion for artwork developed, so did her deepening social awareness. She began teaching in black churches and developed an appreciation for the unique music and worship styles she found there. Leadership roles in her own Presbyterian church led her to travel regularly to New York City, where she enjoyed encounters with ancient and modern forms of art.

The 1940s brought the aftermath of the Great Depression, which was coupled with the Second World War and brought hard economic times to the Connell family. Most of their landholdings were lost to foreclosure.[127]

The loss of the economic security once afforded by the plantation lifestyle propelled Clyde Connell's family into another chapter of history that promoted her success as an artist. A parallel of the Old South way of life still remained at the Caddo Parish Penal Farm. It included one thousand acres of farmland not unlike that worked by tenant families on the Connell family plantation in Belcher. In 1949, T.D. Connell applied for the position of penal farm superintendent, doubtless citing his experience managing a large rural agricultural business of his own. Clyde Connell and her husband moved to the Caddo Parish Penal Farm. The family lived among the inmates, and she worked in an art studio on the farm's grounds. This was one of the most artistically productive periods of her life, and she drew heavily upon the black inmates of the penal farm for inspiration.[128]

The Connells' move to the penal farm perhaps illustrates that the economic ethic of the Old South was still very much alive in the Louisiana prison system at the mid-point of the twentieth century. T.D. Dixon's previous success in running a large commercial cotton plantation provided sufficient career experience for him to function as the warden of a correctional institution. Agricultural experience counted as correctional qualification in Louisiana in the 1940s and is a stark but realistic commentary on the penal farm model.

For the next ten years, Clyde Connell enjoyed the seclusion and security afforded by the penal farm and continued her travels to New York. The 1950s brought abstraction into the mainstream of American artwork, and Connell's visits to the Museum of Modern Art offered artistic inspiration. Her work as a sculptor artist began in earnest at this time, and she enjoyed increasing commercial success and acclaim. Her husband's tenure at the Caddo Parish Penal Farm ended in 1959. Although they left the farm, the memories of her time there remained with her. She often cited it as the significant influence of that period of her life, even in later interviews.[129] Clyde Connell died in 1998. At the time of her death, her works were on display at the Metropolitan Museum of Art in New York.

She always drew inspiration from the places where she lived around the Shreveport area, including that secluded penal farm.[130]

The Caddo Parish Penal Farm closed as a prison facility decades ago and stands abandoned today. Understanding of its history contributes much to the understanding of its ghosts. Perhaps the groans of long-dead convicts echo through the ruins, a site once typical of justice in the South. Whatever might be the source of the haunted legends surrounding the Pea Farm, it will continue to attract those seeking the paranormal. Even if the parish elects to sell the property, the farm's haunted past might end, but its history will endure.

THE MANSFIELD BATTLEFIELD

There is perhaps no more poignant haunted image than that conjured by the ethereal sighting of ghostly Civil War dead, still dressed in blue or gray, armed for the fight yet belonging to a battle that took place in the nineteenth century. In April 1864, the blood of both Union and Confederate soldiers was shed on a remote and rural expanse of Louisiana soil just half an hour from the city limits of Shreveport. The spirits of the dead, either literally or figuratively, will always roam this sacred ground. The Mansfield State Historic Site commemorates their lives and loss. The significance of the battle and the academic and popular interest remains high. Every year, Civil War reenactors and park officials mark the anniversary of the battle, a critical one for the Union's Red River Campaign. Amid the reenactors, it is easy to imagine the ghosts of the fallen soldiers who are said to wander the picturesque battlefield today.

The drive south from Shreveport is a brief and pleasant one, particularly for those who travel there in the spring to commemorate the battle. It can be difficult to imagine the brutality of the bloodshed on what is now a peaceful ground. Even in times of peace, when the sounds of guns and cannon have long ceased, battlefields are places where paranormal activity is often reported.

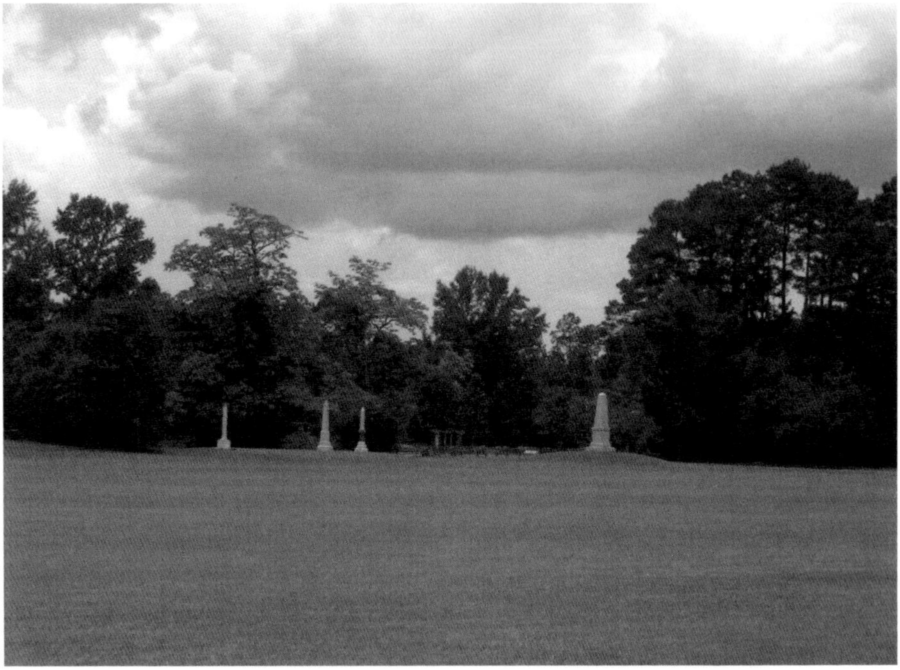

Monuments at Mansfield State Historic Site. *Photograph by Gary D. Joiner.*

Ghost lore includes stories of those who lost their lives suddenly to violence. They are likely to have souls that linger behind in an unsettled earthly existence. Restless spirits such as these have been dramatically shocked from their earthly bodies, and, therefore, battlefields are often reported to be haunted places. The idea of haunted battlefields is not unique to American culture or even unique to the modern era. Accounts from classical antiquity related that for days following battles, the quiet battlefield would resound with the clash of bronze weapons and screams of the dying.[131] Some suggest that battlefields forever carry the imprint of a special kind of psychic energy due to the sheer force of human anguish. Battle reenactors commonly report unusual and unexplained ghostly encounters. Perhaps these reenactors, by the wearing of the uniform of the fallen or by adopting the frame of mind of a long-dead soldier, are more sensitive to the impressions of history left upon the battlefield.[132]

Wars inherently carry with them the burden of loss of life and the destruction of communities and social order. This upheaval is enough to engender nostalgic lore that appropriately romanticizes the heroic fallen. This promotes an undeniable connection to the past that some are reluctant to release. Stories of the haunted battlefield are a creative means of preserving what occurred there not only in the objectivity of history but also in the emotional telling of folklore. In this way, the ghosts of the Mansfield Battlefield work to ensure they are not forgotten nor are the causes or the age in which they lived. The fact that we promote the battlefield ghosts may mirror our inability to confront fully the atrocities of what occurred.

Park officials relate myriad ghost stories, some shared by reenactors and others by visitors to the park. Some have reported seeing faint ghostly images in the early morning and late evening mists at this hallowed site. The images of soldiers wearing either blue or gray move silently, ready for action yet again. Professional paranormal investigations of the Mansfield site by the organization Louisiana Spirits revealed a measurable amount of ghostly activity there. According to that organization, their investigational visit to Mansfield revealed some unusual electromagnetic field reactions, as well as bursts of hot air even on a cold night.[133]

Interpretative Park Ranger Scott Dearman relates the story of a ghostly encounter involving a reenactor that occurred in 2000 during the park's annual Halloween event. A group of three battle reenactors took up positions along a trail for the interactive event. At the end of the night's program, one of them left his station and headed toward a nearby campfire. He saw what he initially believed to be another reenactor, but he noted knee boots worn by the soldier and thought it odd that he had overlooked this authentic uniform detail earlier in the evening. He spoke to the soldier, who did not turn or acknowledge his presence. At that moment, the unnerved reenactor realized that the being near the campfire was not a fellow reenactor but an apparition. Through the years, the experiences of many visitors to the site have produced other reports of ghostly soldiers.

The thread of ghostly apparitions at battlefields and related historic sites is evident across the country. The historic energy of the fallen is imprinted upon these places, and some believe that the presence of reenactors activates that energy in a supernatural sense. Some ghost

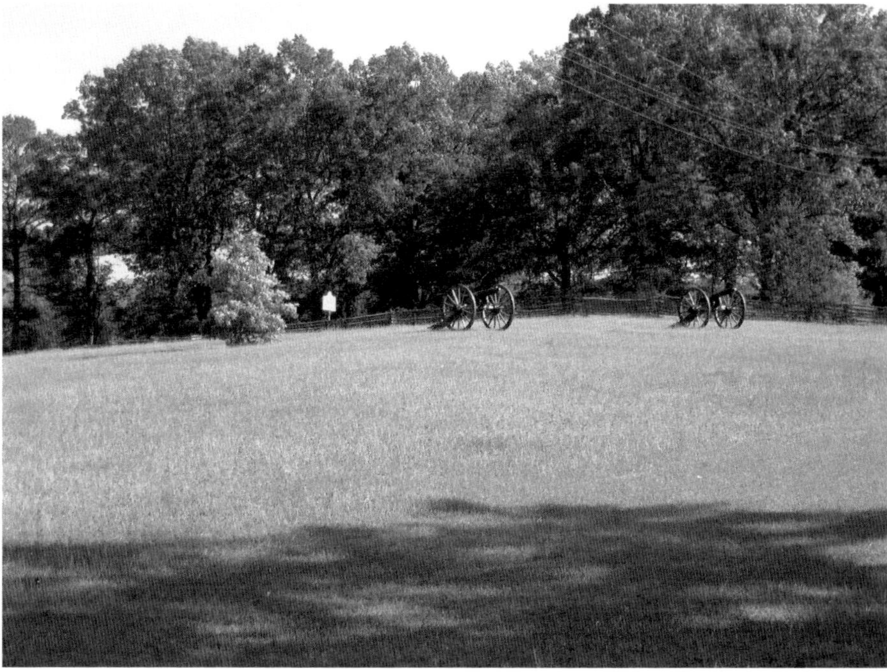

Artillery position on Honeycutt Hill at Mansfield State Historic Site. *Photograph by Gary D. Joiner.*

theorists believe that this energy can only be manifested or known to people who are particularly sensitive or attuned to the possibility and who are interested in the time period or events that shaped the life of the deceased. This idea certainly helps explain the frequent ghost sightings by Civil War reenactors.[134]

The story of the Battle of Mansfield is significantly related to a chapter in the history of Shreveport. The battle was a significant military turning point in Louisiana during the Civil War, as it protected Shreveport from invasion by enemy forces. Shreveport had been made the temporary capital of Louisiana in January 1863 following the fall of New Orleans and the advancement of Union troops throughout southern Louisiana. Louisiana governor Thomas Overton Moore set up offices on Texas Street in downtown Shreveport, and the city's population grew rapidly with its position of state government. A Union offensive focused on northern Louisiana as the gateway to the state of Texas. Union leadership believed that capturing Shreveport, the primary point of concentration for Confederate lieutenant general Edmund Kirby Smith's Trans-Mississippi Department of the Confederacy, would yield both military and political rewards.[135]

General Smith's command headquarters was housed in the 500 block of Spring Street in the heart of the riverfront district of the city, while the bulk of his sixteen thousand men camped just outside the city at Camp Boggs and other locations. During the year prior to the Union army's advance, General Smith ordered the construction of forts and batteries around the city. The first of these was Fort Turnbull, commonly known today as Fort Humbug. This land is currently occupied by the Veteran's Administration hospital. The others were Fort Jenkins and Fort Albert Sidney Johnson, located strategically around the downtown area. Other defenses linked these forts. Still others were located in Bossier Parish opposite Shreveport. In all, the defenses comprised four major forts, three minor forts, twelve named artillery positions and three unnamed artillery positions. This defensive posturing on the part of the Trans-Mississippi Department reflects the very real military danger facing Shreveport.

With the fall of Vicksburg, Mississippi, and Port Hudson, Louisiana, in July 1863, Union forces completely controlled the Mississippi River. The Union high command decided that Texas would be the next objective in the Trans-Mississippi area, and the Red River was a logical strategic choice for the approach. A joint army-navy advance was planned, with approximately thirty-five thousand troops under the command of General Nathaniel P. Banks and a naval fleet commanded by David Porter. From March 10, 1864, until May 22, 1864, the Union waged its Red River Campaign and gained nothing significant, but it did suffer severe losses of men, time and resources.

Why was a campaign directed at Texas? The Union command believed that a successful Red River campaign would accomplish several important objectives for the overall war effort. First, cotton was a prized commodity in New England textile mills. The need for cotton made Shreveport a vulnerable target, since by this time cotton trading dominated the port's activity. Also, Union success in Shreveport would deter a joint French-Mexican force and supplies from reaching the Confederate army in

Louisiana. Perhaps most important was the belief that the campaign would succeed in bringing both Texas and Louisiana back into the Union, since Union forces already occupied the major port city of New Orleans.

Of all the motivating factors for the campaign, cotton may have been the most crucial. By the beginning of 1862, Northern textile mills had nearly ground to a halt due to a cotton shortage. This threatened not only the industrial economy of the cotton manufacturing regions but also the supplies of cloth necessary to maintain and supply the Union army in the field with everything from uniforms to bandages. The occupation of New Orleans had actually yielded little in terms of cotton. Records reveal that only twenty-seven thousand bales of cotton were confiscated from New Orleans in 1862, compared to nearly two million bales that were available in the city in 1861.[136] This must have been a significant disappointment to the Union command and the Lincoln administration, and it likely contributed to the urgency of the Red River Campaign.

Observers believed that Texas was capable of producing large quantities of cotton for the Union. Securing its readmission would bring a solution to the crisis. Union officials were concerned with the control of the major waterway, the Mississippi River, as a first line of strategy. This meant that the campaign directed at Texas had to be delayed until Union forces secured the Mississippi River. If the cotton situation in the North was desperate in 1862, it was critical by early 1864, when the Red River Campaign began.

In late January 1864, Union major general Nathaniel Prentiss Banks, commanding the Army of the Gulf in New Orleans, received word that the Red River area of Louisiana contained large amounts of stored cotton that belonged to the government of the Confederacy. Banks also had intelligence indicating that some Confederates were willing to ensure the safety of the cotton if the Union forces advanced, providing they could expect financial rewards. This would have been in direct violation of a Confederate statute that required the destruction of cotton as a last resort to keep it out of Union hands.[137]

Aside from the promise of large supplies of cotton, the Red River Campaign held promise that it could influence the presidential election in the fall of 1864. Cotton and politics are inseparable. Renewed shipments of cotton to Northern mills would help lessen severe economic deficits and unemployment, and that, in turn, would be a favorable achievement for the Lincoln administration. The Confederate military recognized the relationship between cotton and presidential politics and began to prepare for the possibility of Union invasion well in advance.

The year of the campaign posed equally desperate challenges for the Confederates as well, particularly after the fall of Gettysburg and Vicksburg. The supply lines stopped in Louisiana after Vicksburg fell. The flow of arms from the east was severed when Union forces occupied that key stronghold on the Mississippi River. The Confederate command realized that Shreveport was on the short list of desirable targets, since most of the remainder of Louisiana was already under Union control. At the apex of these converging military forces was the tiny community of Mansfield. In 1864, it was all that stood between the Union army and the capital city of Shreveport.

Following the Red River in early spring of 1864, the Union army and naval forces reached the small settlement of Natchitoches without facing Confederate opposition of any significance. At Natchitoches, the Union army left the route alongside the Red River and marched toward Shreveport on a rural road that passed the small town of Mansfield. Abandoning the river and the support of the Union navy was one of many tactical blunders on the part of General Banks. With a series of successful maneuvers on the part of General Richard Taylor (son of U.S. president Zachary Taylor), the Confederate army rallied to stop the Union's plans to capture Shreveport and, ultimately, Texas.

Following a two-hour cavalry engagement with Union forces near Wilson's Farm on April 7, 1864, General Taylor took a defensive position about four miles south of the town of Mansfield, where the state historic site and park are now located. General Banks was not expecting a fight. His army was jammed into a single narrow column about thirty miles long. Most of his forces could not join in the battle. General Taylor took advantage of this, since these deficiencies proved to be helpful to the Confederate forces, which were heavily outnumbered.

Thus, the Battle of Mansfield became the central and key battle in a two-month campaign to gain the strategic positions in the Red River valley. Late in the afternoon of April 8, General Taylor decided to attack both Union flanks. Heavy casualties ensued for both sides, and General Banks withdrew. On the following day, General Banks met General Taylor yet again at Pleasant Hill. Together, the Battles of Mansfield and Pleasant Hill represented decisive Confederate victories and prevented the planned Union invasion of Texas. Further, they stopped the Union advance on the city of Shreveport. Shreveport's role in this chapter of history was protected, and it remained the capital of Confederate Louisiana until June 1865. Isolated from news of the events in the eastern theatre of the war, the Trans-Mississippi actions continued even after Robert E. Lee surrendered to General Ulysses Grant.

The Mansfield battleground has no exclusivity on haunting by Civil War dead. The conflict cost some 600,000 lives, and numerous roads, bridges, pasturelands, mountain passes and buildings across this country witnessed the brutality of battle. No other event in United States history has produced more ghost stories. The most famous comes from Gettysburg, Pennsylvania, where 43,500 men were casualties over the course of three days of fighting in July 1863.[138] Legend has it that the ghost of George Washington appeared during the height of the battle, drew his sword and led Confederate soldiers up a hill known as "Little Round Top."[139] Many residents of Maryland recount a legend along State's Route 116. Every year during the anniversary of Gettysburg, residents report seeing phantom horse-drawn wagons carrying the dead, with wounded Confederate soldiers as a prominent feature of the story.[140] These two examples from hundreds of such ghost stories reinforce the relationship of Civil War battlefields across the country with paranormal encounters.

NOTES

Introduction

1. Bryant, *Handbook of Death*, 90.
2. Ibid.
3. Senate Document, "Report from Superintendent of Western River Improvements."

Oakland Cemetery

4. Newberry, "Oakland Cemetery," 3.
5. Bill Bowen, "Here Lies History," *Shreveport Journal*, April 27, 1990, 5-B. Louisiana State University at Shreveport Noel Memorial Library, Archives and Special Collections, Vertical File (Cemeteries).
6. Although the historic marker on the yellow fever mound states 759 dead, this figure comes from the November 15, 1873 tabulation in the *Shreveport Times*. Using the daily tallies between August 20, 1873, and November 12, 1873, 715 bodies were interred within the mound. Additionally, approximately 75 other graves have been identified

under marked monuments within the cemetery. Others are very likely as well.

7. Thomson, *Historic Shreveport*, 30.
8. Belanger, *Ghost Files*, 35.
9. Rule, *Ghosts Among Us*, 155.
10. Holy Trinity Catholic Church, "Yellow Fever Epidemic of 1873."
11. *American Journal of the Medical Sciences*, "Report of the Committee on the Yellow Fever Epidemic," 480–82.
12. Ibid.
13. Ibid.
14. Carrigan, "Impact of Epidemic Yellow Fever," 5.
15. Crosby, *American Plague*, 12.
16. "Yellow Fever," Department of Health and Human Services.
17. *New York Times*, "How Burials Are Made in Shreveport—The Disease Imported from Cuba and Appeal to the People," September 30, 1873.
18. Ibid.
19. Carrigan, "Impact of Epidemic Yellow Fever," 22.
20. *American Journal of the Medical Sciences*, "Report of the Committee on the Yellow Fever Epidemic."

MUNICIPAL AUDITORIUM

21. Aswell, *Louisiana Rocks!*, 265.
22. Ibid., 272.
23. Laird, *Louisiana Hayride*, 7.
24. Ibid., 8.
25. John Andrew Prime, "The Muni," *Shreveport Times*, March 3, 1985, 10F–12F.
26. Thomas interview, September 29, 2009.
27. Ibid. (Electronic voice phenomena recordings are found as digital media files on the Louisiana Spirits website at www.laspirits.com.)
28. Discovery Channel, http://dsc.discovery.com/tv/ghost-lab/ghost-lab.html.

29. Discovery Channel, http://dsc.discovery.com/videos/ghost-lab-audio-evidence.html?smid=FBGST-FWP-VAP.
30. National Park Service, www.nps.gov.

C.E. Byrd High School

31. McLaurin, *Glimpses of the City of Byrd*, 47.
32. Cubberly, *Public Education in the United States*, 131.
33. McLaurin, *Glimpses of the City of Byrd*, 4.
34. O'Pry, *Chronicles of Shreveport*, 338.
35. Ibid.
36. McLaurin, *Glimpses of the City of Byrd*, 5.
37. Ibid., 7.
38. Ibid., 9.
39. Parent, *Inside the Carnival*, 125.
40. McLaurin, *Glimpses of the City of Byrd*, 12.
41. Williams, "Anti-Semitism and Shreveport," 387–98.
42. McLaurin, *Glimpses of the City of Byrd*, 19.
43. Ibid., 51.
44. Blackman, *Field Guide to North American Hauntings*, 86.
45. McLaurin, *Glimpses of the City of Byrd*, 63.
46. Ibid., 71.
47. Ibid., 89.
48. Bankston and Caldas, *A Troubled Dream*, 173.
49. Ibid., 139.
50. Coroner's Report of Death, Shreveport Police Department Investigative Report, from the Dr. Willis P. Butler Collection, Louisiana State University at Shreveport, Noel Archives and Special Collections.
51. McLaurin, *Glimpses of the City of Byrd*, 162.

Dr. Willis Butler

52. Butler, *Will Somebody Call the Coroner?*, 52–53.
53. Meador, *Inventory and Guide to Willis P. Butler Collection.*
54. Ibid.
55. Bob Mahoney, "Sympathy Marked Doctor's Treatment of Drug Addicts," *Shreveport Journal*, October 18, 1966.
56. Butler, "Public Health Problem of Narcotic Drug Addiction," 164.
57. Mahoney, "Sympathy Marked Doctor's Treatment of Drug Addicts."
58. Aurin, "Chasing the Dragon," 417.
59. Ibid.
60. Ibid., 419.
61. Ibid., 423.
62. Ibid., 425.
63. Becker, *Outsiders*, 137.
64. Marge Fischer, "Treating Drug Addicts in a Humane Way," *Shreveport Journal*, June 24, 1988.
65. Butler, *Will Somebody Call the Coroner?*, 164.
66. Ibid.
67. Ibid.
68. Fischer, "Treating Drug Addicts in a Humane Way."
69. Meador, *Inventory and Guide to Willis P. Butler Collection.*
70. Obituary, "Pioneering Coroner Dr. Willis Butler Dies at 103," *Shreveport Times*, June 11, 1991.
71. Butler, *Will Somebody Call the Coroner?*, 68.

The Logan Mansion

72. Obituary of Lafayette Robert Logan, *Shreveport Times*, September 22,1919.
73. U.S. Department of Commerce, Twelfth Decennial Census (1900), Caddo Parish, Louisiana. Washington, D.C.: Unpublished tabulations in the National Archives and Records Administration.
74. Ibid.

75. Ibid.
76. Obituary of Lafayette Robert Logan, *Shreveport Times*, September 22, 1919.
77. "Directory of Deceased American Physicians, 1804–1929."
78. Twelfth Decennial Census (1900), Caddo Parish, Louisiana.
79. Obituary of Wade Hampton, *Shreveport Times*, May 29, 1952.
80. *Shreveport Times*, "Old Mansion Renovated by KCOZ," December 9, 1976.
81. Thomas, interview, August 12, 2009.
82. "Logan Mansion," Louisiana Spirits Paranormal Investigations.
83. Death Certificate for Theodora Hunt, Arkansas History Commission.

The Davis Homeplace

84. McLaurin, *Glimpses of the City of Byrd*, 22.
85. U.S. Department of Commerce, Seventh Decennial Census (1850), Jefferson County, Mississippi. Washington, D.C.: Unpublished tabulations in the National Archives and Records Administration.
86. Kane, *Natchez on the Mississippi*, 174.
87. Ibid., 176.
88. General Land Office Records, Bureau of Land Management.
89. Kane, *Natchez on the Mississippi*, 177.
90. Ibid., 179.
91. U.S. Department of Commerce, Eighth Decennial Census (1860), Jefferson County, Mississippi. Washington, D.C.: Unpublished tabulations in the National Archives and Records Administration.
92. Kane, *Natchez on the Mississippi*, 183.
93. *Biographical and Historical Memoirs of Louisiana*, 273–74.
94. Neagles, *Confederate Research Sources*, 1019.
95. U.S. Department of Commerce, Thirteenth Decennial Census (1910), Caddo Parish, Louisiana. Washington, D.C.: Unpublished tabulations in the National Archives and Records Administration.
96. "William Dickinson Dalzell," *Dictionary of the Louisiana Historical Association*.

97. "The Clergy of St. Mark's." St. Mark's Episcopal Church, San Antonio, Texas, www.stmarks-sa.org. Accessed March 10, 2010.
98. "William Dickinson Dalzell," *Dictionary of the Louisiana Historical Association*.
99. Twelfth Decennial Census (1900), Caddo Parish, Louisiana.
100. U.S. Department of Commerce, Tenth Decennial Census (1880), Mobile County, Alabama. Washington, D.C.: Unpublished tabulations in the National Archives and Records Administration.
101. Sabol, *Ghost Culture*, 115.

THE FORBING GHOST

102. Ramsland, 362.
103. United States Veterans Schedule, 1890; U.S. Civil War Records and Profiles, Historical Data Systems.
104. *Southern Reporter*, 203–4.
105. U.S. Department of Commerce, Tenth Decennial Census (1880), Caddo Parish, Louisiana. Washington, D.C.: Unpublished tabulations in the National Archives and Records Administration.
106. U.S. Department of Commerce, Thirteenth Decennial Census (1910), Caddo Parish, Louisiana. Washington, D.C.: Unpublished tabulations in the National Archives and Records Administration.
107. Map of Caddo Parish and Bossier Parish with Portions of Webster, DeSoto and Red River Parishes.
108. Estaville, *Confederate Neckties*, 62; "Railroads," Parish of Caddo.
109. *Shreveport Journal*, "Forbing Ghost Still Spooks Local Folks," October 27, 1984, 1B.
110. Ogden, *Haunted Highways*, 180.
111. *TIME* magazine, "Transport: Awfullest Thing," December 1, 1938.
112. Brown, *Haunted Places in the American South*, 237–38.
113. Ogden, *Haunted Highways*, 222.
114. Reevy, *Ghost Train*, 137.

THE CADDO PARISH PENAL FARM

115. Carleton, *Politics and Punishment*, 14.
116. Zimmerman, "Penal Reform Movement in the South," 462–92.
117. Haynes, *American Prison System*, 173.
118. Feldman and Ingham, *African American Business Leaders*, 32.
119. Compiled Military Service Records of Volunteer Union Soldiers Who Served with the United States Colored Troops: 55th Massachusetts Infantry (Colored).
120. U.S. Department of Commerce, Ninth Decennial Census (1870), Caddo Parish, Louisiana. Washington, D.C.: Unpublished tabulations in the National Archives and Records Administration.
121. Feldman and Ingham, *African American Business Leaders*, 33.
122. Ibid., 34.
123. Ibid.
124. Obituary, C.C. Antoine, *Shreveport Journal*, September 14, 1921.
125. John Andrew Prime, "Hand in Hand for History."
126. Moser, *Clyde Connell*, 18–19.
127. Ibid., 23.
128. Ibid, 24–25.
129. Lynn Randolph, "Clyde Connell."
130. Robert A. Smith, Obituary, "Clyde Connell: Sculptor Inspired by Louisiana Bayous," *New York Times*, May 10, 1998.

THE MANSFIELD BATTLEFIELD

131. Felton, *Haunted Greece and Rome*, 17.
132. Belanger, *Ghosts of War*, 17.
133. Louisiana Spirits Paranormal Investigations Report, April 18, 2010.
134. Kachuba, *Ghosthunters*, 169.
135. Evans, *Confederate Military History*, 133.
136. Johnson, *Red River Campaign*, 13.

137. Ibid., 53.
138. Fox, *Regimental Losses in the American Civil War.*
139. Cochran and Wetzel, *Haunted U.S.A.*, 17.
140. Ibid., 20.

BIBLIOGRAPHY

Manuscripts

Willis P. Butler Collection, Louisiana State University at Shreveport Noel Memorial Library Archives and Special Collection.

Books and Periodicals

American Journal of the Medical Sciences. "Report of the Committee on the Yellow Fever Epidemic of 1873 of Shreveport, Louisiana." 66, issue 134 (April 1874).

Aswell, Tom. *Louisiana Rocks! The True Genesis of Rock and Roll.* Gretna, LA: Pelican Publishing, 2010.

Aurin, Marcus. "Chasing the Dragon: The Cultural Metamorphosis of Opium in the United States, 1825–1935." *Medical Anthropology Quarterly* 14, no. 3 (September 2000).

Bankston, Carl Leon, and Stephen J. Caldas. *A Troubled Dream: The Promise and Failure of School Desegregation in Louisiana.* Nashville, TN: Vanderbilt University Press, 2002.

Becker, Howard S. *Outsiders: Studies in the Sociology of Deviance*. New York: Simon and Schuster, 1997.

Belanger, Jeff. *The Ghost Files: Paranormal Encounters, Discussion and Research*. Franklin Lakes, NJ: Career Press, 2007.

———. *Ghosts of War*. New York: Rosen Publishing, 2009.

Biographical and Historical Memoirs of Louisiana. Vol. 2. Chicago: Goodspeed Publishing, 1892.

Blackman, W. Haden. *The Field Guide to North American Hauntings*. Indianapolis, IN: Three Rivers Press, 1998.

Brown, Alan. *Haunted Places in the American South*. Jackson: University of Mississippi Press, 2002.

Bryant, Clifton. *Handbook of Death and Dying*. London: Sage Publications, 2003.

Butler, Willis P. "How One American City Is Meeting the Public Health Problem of Narcotic Drug Addiction." *American Medicine* 17, no. 3 (March 1922).

———. *Will Somebody Call the Coroner?* Shreveport, LA: Ritz Publications, 2007.

Carleton, Mark T. *Politics and Punishment: The History of the Louisiana State Penal System*. Baton Rouge: Louisiana State University Press, 1971.

Carrigan, Jo Ann. "Impact of Epidemic Yellow Fever on Life in Louisiana." *Louisiana History: The Journal of the Louisiana Historical Association* 4, no. 1 (Winter 1963).

Cochran, Josh, and Charles Wetzel. *Haunted U.S.A.* New York: Sterling Publishing, 2008.

Crosby, Molly Caldwell. *The American Plague: The Untold Story of Yellow Fever, the Epidemic that Shaped Our History*. New York: Berkley Publishing Group, 2006.

Cubberly, E.P. *Public Education in the United States: A Study and Interpretation of American Educational History*. New York: Houghton Mifflin, 1919.

Estaville, Lawrence E., Jr. *Confederate Neckties: Louisiana Railroads in the Civil War*. Ruston, LA: McGinty Publications, 1989.

Evans, Clement Anselm. *Confederate Military History*. Boston: Harvard University Press, 1899.

Feldman, Lynne, and John Ingham. *African American Business Leaders: A Biographical Dictionary*. Westport, CT: Greenwood Press, 1994.

Felton, David. *Haunted Greece and Rome: Ghost Stories from Classical Antiquity*. Austin: University of Texas Press, 1998.

Fox, William E. *Regimental Losses in the American Civil War: A Treatise on the Extent and Nature of the Mortuary Losses in the Union Regiments, with Full and Exhaustive Statistics Compiled from the Official Records on File in the State Militaries Bureaus and at Washington*. Dayton, OH: Morningside Bookshop Press, 1993.

Haynes, Frederick E. *The American Prison System*. New York: McGraw Hill, 1939.

Johnson, Ludwell. *Red River Campaign: Politics and Cotton in the Civil War*. Kent, OH: Kent University Press, 1993.

Kachuba, John. *Ghosthunters: On the Trail of Mediums, Dowsers, Spirit Seekers and Other Investigators of America's Paranormal World*. Franklin Lakes, NJ: Career Books, 2007.

Kane, Harnett. *Natchez on the Mississippi*. New York: William Morrow and Company, 1947.

Laird, Tracey E.W. *Louisiana Hayride: Louisiana and Roots Music Along the Red River*. New York: Oxford University Press, 2005.

McLaurin, Ann. *Glimpses of the City of Byrd, 1925–1995*. Shreveport: self-published, 1995.

Meador, Patricia. *Inventory and Guide to Willis P. Butler Collection, Louisiana State University at Shreveport Noel Library Archives and Special Collections*. 1979.

Moser, Charlotte. *Clyde Connell: The Life and Art of a Louisiana Woman*. Austin: University of Texas Press, 1988.

Neagles, James C. *Confederate Research Sources: A Guide to Archive Collections*. Vol. 2. Salt Lake City, UT: Ancestry, Inc., 1986,

Newberry, Jane. "Oakland Cemetery: Its Trials and Tribulations—The Evolution of a National Historic Landmark." *North Louisiana Historical Association Journal* 19, no. 2.

Ogden, Thomas. *Haunted Highways: Spooky Stories, Strange Happenings and Supernatural Sightings*. New York: Globe Publishing, 2008.

O'Pry, Maude Hearn. *Chronicles of Shreveport and Caddo Parish*. Shreveport, LA: Journal Printing Co., 1928.

Parent, Wayne. *Inside the Carnival: Unmasking Louisiana Politics*. Baton Rouge: Louisiana State University Press, 2006.

Ramsland, Katherine. *Ghost: A Firsthand Account into the World of Paranormal Activity*. New York: St. Martin's Press, 2001.

Randolph, Lynn. "Clyde Connell." *National Women's Caucus for Art Conference Biography*. Los Angeles, CA: 1985.

Reevy, Tony. *Ghost Train: American Railroad Ghost Legends*. Lynchburg, VA: TLC Publishing, 1998.

Rule, Leslie. *Ghosts Among Us: True Stories of Spirit Encounters*. New York: Andrews McNeel Publishing, 2004.

Sabol, John. *Ghost Culture: Theories, Context and Scientific Practice*. Bloomington, IN: Authorhouse, 2007.

Southern Reporter. Eagan, MN: West Publishing, Volume 3.

Thomson, Bailey. *Historic Shreveport: A Guide*. Shreveport, LA: Shreveport Journal Publishing Co., 1980.

Williams, Beverly S. "Anti-Semitism and Shreveport, Louisiana: The Situation in the 1920s." *Louisiana History: The Journal of the Louisiana Historical Society* 21, no. 4 (Autumn 1980).

Zimmerman, Jane. "The Penal Reform Movement in the South During the Progressive Era, 1890–1917." *Journal of Southern History* 17, no. 4 (November 1951).

Newspapers

New York Times, September 30, 1873; May 10, 1988.

Shreveport Journal, April 27, 1900; September 14, 1921; October 18, 1966; October 27, 1984; June 24, 1988.

Shreveport Times, September 22, 1919; May 29, 1952; December 9, 1976; March 3, 1985; June 11, 1991.

GOVERNMENT DOCUMENTS

Compiled Military Service Records of Volunteer Union Soldiers Who Served with the United States Colored Troops: 55th Massachusetts Infantry (Colored). National Archives Microfilm Publication M1801, 16 rolls. Records of the Adjutant General's Office, 1780s–1917, Record Group 94. National Archives, Washington, D.C.

United States Congress, Senate. "Report from Superintendent of Western River Improvements." 26th Congress, 2nd Session, 1840.

U.S. Department of Commerce, Eighth Decennial Census (1860), Jefferson County, Mississippi. Washington, D.C.: Unpublished tabulations in the National Archives and Records Administration. Accessed from United States Census 1860; Police District 4, Jefferson, Mississippi; Roll M653_584; Page 610; Image 32; Family History Library, Film 803584.

U.S. Department of Commerce, Ninth Decennial Census (1870), Caddo Parish, Louisiana. Washington, D.C.: Unpublished tabulations in the National Archives and Records Administration. Acquired at United States Census, 1870; Census Place Shreveport, Caddo, Louisiana; Roll M593_508; Page 528B; Image 470; Family History Library Film 552007.

U.S. Department of Commerce, Seventh Decennial Census (1850), Jefferson County, Mississippi. Washington, D.C.: Unpublished tabulations in the National Archives and Records Administration.

U.S. Department of Commerce, Tenth Decennial Census (1880), Caddo Parish, Louisiana. Washington, D.C.: Unpublished tabulations in the National Archives and Records Administration.

U.S. Department of Commerce, Tenth Decennial Census (1880), Mobile County, Alabama. Washington, D.C.: Unpublished tabulations in the National Archives and Records Administration. Accessed through United States Census, 1880; Census Place Mobile, Alabama; Roll T9_25; Family History; Film 1254025; Page 287.3000; Enumeration District 136; Image 0296.

U.S. Department of Commerce, Thirteenth Decennial Census (1910), Caddo Parish, Louisiana. Washington, D.C.: Unpublished tabulations in the National Archives and Records Administration. Accessed from 1910 United States Census; Shreveport Ward 6, Caddo, Louisiana; Roll T624_510; Page: 1B; Enumeration District 46; Image 466.

U.S. Department of Commerce, Twelfth Decennial Census (1900), Caddo Parish, Louisiana. Washington, D.C.: Unpublished tabulations in the National Archives and Records Administration.

MAPS

Map of Caddo Parish and Bossier Parish with Portions of Webster, DeSoto and Red River Parishes, State of Louisiana, 1930, prepared by the Caddo Parish Highway Department and the Bossier Parish Highway Department. Archives and Special Collections, Noel Memorial Library, Louisiana State University in Shreveport.

INTERNET SOURCES

"The Clergy of St. Mark's." St. Mark's Episcopal Church, San Antonio, Texas. www.stmarks-sa.org.

"Clyde Connell." *National Women's Caucus for Art Conference Biography*. Los Angeles, 1985. www.nationalwca.org.

Death Certificate for Theodora Hunt, Arkansas History Commission. www.ark-ives.com.

"Directory of Deceased American Physicians, 1804–1929." http://openlibrary.org/books/OL1503158M/Directory_of_deceased_American_physicians_1804-1929.

Discovery Channel. *Ghost Lab* official website. http://dsc.discovery.com/tv/ghost-lab/ghost-lab.html.

———. *Ghost Lab*. http://dsc.discovery.com/videos/ghost-lab-audio-evidence.html?smid=FBGST-FWP-VAP.

General Land Office Records, Bureau of Land Management. http://www.glorecords.blm.gov.

Holy Trinity Catholic Church. "Yellow Fever Epidemic of 1873." http://www.holytrinity-shreveport.com.

"Logan Mansion." Louisiana Spirits Paranormal Investigations. www.laspirits.com.

National Park Service. www.nps.org.

Parish of Caddo. "Railroads." www.caddohistory.com/railroads.html.

Prime, John Andrew. "Hand in Hand for History." http://home.earthlink.net/~japrime/cwrt/antoine.htm.

TIME magazine. "Transport: Awfullest Thing," December 1, 1938. http://www.time.com/time/magazine/article/0,9171,760486,00.html.

United States Veterans Schedules, 1890; U.S. Civil War Records and Profiles, Historical Data Systems. http://search.ancestry.com/search/db.aspx?dbid=8667

"William Dickinson Dalzell." *Dictionary of the Louisiana Historical Association.* www.lahistory.org

"Yellow Fever." Department of Health and Human Services, Centers for Disease Control and Prevention. http://www.cdc.gov/ncidod/diseases/submenus/sub_yellow_fever.htm.

INTERVIEWS

Thomas, Brandon. Louisiana Spirits Paranormal Investigations, interview. Shreveport, Louisiana, August 12, 2009; September 29, 2009.

ABOUT THE AUTHORS

Gary Joiner is a history professor at LSU–Shreveport, director of the Red River Regional Studies Center and has written many articles and books on the history of the Red River Valley region of northwestern Louisiana. Since 2006, he has aired a weekly radio program called *History Matters* for Red River Radio and is an experienced and popular lecturer on history, geography and archaeology. His myriad affiliations include the Civil War Preservation Trust, U.S.; the North Louisiana Historical Association (former board of directors, former editor of *North Louisiana History*); the DeSoto Parish Historical Society (former president); the Southern Historical Association; the Louisiana Historical Association; the Oakland Cemetery Preservation Society; the Spring Street Historical Museum; Red River Radio; the Red River Heritage Association; the Sons and Daughters of Pioneer River Men; and the Historic Shreveport Preservation Society.

Cheryl H. White, PhD, is assistant professor of history at Louisiana State University at Shreveport and holds the endowed Hubert Humpreys Professorship. A winner of numerous teaching awards, Dr. White is a national and regional speaker and lecturer. She has founded community initiatives aimed at bringing arts and culture to underserved youth and has developed history-based reading projects for adult learners. Her publications and numerous professional presentations include topics related to local history, religious history and early modern England.